QUALITY WITH A GRIN

EMBRACING HUMOR AND INNOVATION
IN QUALITY MANAGEMENT

Selda Nur Simsir

ISBN: 9798860062238
Cover design by: Seyda Simsir

To my beloved family,

This book is dedicated to you with profound gratitude and deep love. Your unwavering commitment to the principle of 'doing the right thing all the time, even when no one is watching' has not only shaped my character but also guided my path in the realm of quality management. Your lessons of integrity, honesty, and resilience have been my foundation, and I am endlessly thankful for the values you've instilled in me.

As I journeyed into the world of quality, your teachings illuminated my way, reminding me that excellence and ethical conduct are not just professional ideals but an extension of the values we hold dear. Your support, though rooted in different life experiences, has been a steady anchor, inspiring me to explore innovative approaches and
embrace laughter in the pursuit of quality.
With profound respect and appreciation,

S. Nur Simsir

Table of Contents

Introduction

In the realm of quality management, precision and meticulous attention to detail are the guiding principles. Regulations, protocols, and standards weave a tapestry that often seems to leave no room for frivolity. Quality, after all, is a serious business, and rightfully so. The stakes are high, the consequences substantial. Yet, in the heart of this seriousness, there lies a powerful ally that is often underestimated and overlooked: humour.

Imagine for a moment a workplace where laughter is as common as emails, and humour is as valued as precision. It's not an image that readily comes to mind when thinking about the critical world of quality management. However, this book is here to challenge that perception, to introduce a different perspective—one that suggests that embracing humour is not just an escape from the pressure, but a strategic approach to enhancing quality, innovation, and camaraderie.

Welcome to "Quality with a Grin: Embracing Humour and Innovation in Quality Management." In the following chapters, we will embark on a journey that explores the unconventional, the unexpected, and the often uncharted territory of humour in the context of quality. This journey is inspired by real-life experiences, where laughter defused tension, where innovation blossomed amidst jokes, and where a shared chuckle became the glue that held teams together.

But why humour? Isn't quality management about rigid adherence to rules, stern faces, and the occasional sternly-worded email? It is, and it isn't. This book invites you to discover the untapped potential of humour in navigating the complexities of quality management. The humour we speak of isn't about trivializing serious matters; rather, it's about infusing an atmosphere of positivity that fuels creativity, encourages resilience, and makes even the most challenging aspects of quality management a bit more manageable.

As you journey through the pages ahead, you'll encounter stories of mishaps and triumphs, of unexpected twists that left professionals rolling with laughter. You'll explore how humour isn't just a remedy for stress; it's a catalyst for innovative problem-solving, effective leadership, and a more engaging workplace. You'll meet

2

the "Quality Jester," the embodiment of a light-hearted approach to quality control that proves quality doesn't have to be somber.

In this book, you'll discover that humour and innovation are not mutually exclusive, but rather they go hand in hand. By the end of our journey, you might just find yourself considering how a well-timed joke could be as essential to your quality management toolkit as any regulation or guideline.

So, whether you're a seasoned quality management professional or someone just stepping into this world, join us in this exploration of how a smile can transform the way we approach quality. Let's embark on a journey that proves that quality with a grin is not just a whimsical notion, but a strategic advantage in the quest for excellence.

Let's begin our adventure, where laughter and quality management come together in a harmony that's both enlightening and entertaining.

Chapter 1: The Humorous Prelude: Embracing Laughter on the Quality Journey

> *"Laughter is the shortest distance between two people." - Victor Borge*

In the world of quality management, where meticulous attention to detail is paramount, it's easy to get caught up in the seriousness of everything. Quality management often comes with rules and regulations, creating an environment that seems inherently serious and focused on risks. However, let's start this book on a lighter note with a story that sets the stage for the importance of humour in our journey to quality.

Imagine a quality manager who tirelessly worked on a process improvement project and proudly presents the meticulously prepared report to the team. They begin the presentation with an air of anticipation, only to realize that the pages of the report are oddly disorganized. It's as if the document has taken on a life of its own, engaging in a whimsical dance of disorder. With a smile, they say, "It seems our report has decided to demonstrate the importance of adaptability and unexpected surprises! Let's embrace this comical moment and find joy in our journey towards quality excellence."

This incident serves as a reminder that even in the most meticulous processes of life, there's a way to create laughter and unexpected surprises. Embracing these moments not only reduces stress but also fosters an environment of creativity, camaraderie, and resilience.

As you read this book, consider how you'd feel if this happened to you. This book highlights the importance of adopting fun approaches to alleviate stress in quality management. This introductory story emphasizes that quality is often subject to unexpected moments and underscores the significance of our approach in such situations. The book is valuable for its concrete examples of a subject many need. As a quality management professional, I know I excel in innovative approaches, but humour has never been my forte. Yet, I've learned its essential nature in my journey. I invite you to contemplate moments when you feel similarly.

So, fasten your seatbelts and prepare for a journey of discovering the amusing and insightful aspects of quality management, grinning leadership, and stress reduction techniques. Together, we'll explore a new perspective, consider how process management could be with a fun leader, reflect on the positive effects of humour on operational processes, and ponder personal development points. Leave judgments and conventional thought systems behind for this exploratory journey into the world of utopian and comical stories—wondering how things might have been.

And so, dear readers, let this journey remind you that sometimes the funniest moments arise from life's unexpected twists and turns. With humour, determination, and a commitment to quality, we can navigate the occasional absurdities of the workplace and achieve success in delightful ways.

Elevate this journey with laughter, insight, and wit! Get ready to explore the comedic side of quality management and unleash your inner quality jester as we embark on this journey together. Adding humour is an essential part of serious quality management. While we flip through these pages, remember that embracing innovative approaches, including humour, is a step toward success.

Chapter 2: The Quality Jester: A Comedic Approach to Quality Control

In the serious world of quality control, where meticulous attention to detail is paramount, there exists a hidden hero: the Quality Jester. This section explores the role of the Quality Jester and how a comedic approach can bring laughter and lightness to the realm of quality control.

Let me emphasize the need for this approach. Can anyone deny the healing and soothing power of humour? Let's invite those who do to be a bit more flexible :) Laughter is one of the strongest remedies. In environments where stress is high, a lack of flexibility and laughter can fuel negativity. It's somewhat ironic that we rarely see much in the way of awareness activities in the workplace. Training that separates humour from processes or injects a few jokes serves as an example of how we strive to maintain composure in serious environments, where laughter is seen as a non-work activity. But wouldn't you want to have a risk management meeting full of laughter? Imagine having a meeting room where each risk point isn't seen as a source of stress, but rather a source of amusement, notes like "What happened this month?" and "Don't do it again!" And don't forget to add a chuckle while mentioning last year's archive-raccoon antics. Isn't it fun? In a world where we all need a good laugh, let's consider managing quality and leadership with plenty of laughter. The story of a thieving mouse overdosing on medicine from the medicine cabinet isn't just sad and stressful; it's a bit funny too. Quality management has the potential to be not only the subject of bafflement for the uninitiated but also a topic that can reduce stress and increase enjoyment. Have we posted a sign in the pharmacy that says, "Unauthorized personnel and mice not allowed"? I find all this instructive humour quite amusing. Just thinking about it makes me happy. This is why the Quality Jester is so important. Let's discover the "quality clown" within us. Don't get caught up in exaggerations. Take a look at learning!

This book is written to encourage a bit of different thinking and to foster innovative thought. The Quality Jester knows that humour has a place in quality management. They believe that a carefree perspective can improve problem-solving, boost team morale, and nurture creativity in a quality-focused environment.

This section highlights how enjoying quality inspections can transform them from mundane tasks into opportunities for fun, using entertaining anecdotes and unexpected encounters. The Quality Jester shows us that even in the most challenging processes, laughter can create a more positive and productive atmosphere.

As quality managers strive to balance multiple responsibilities, they can learn from the art of juggling. This section explores the parallels between quality management and skilful juggling, sharing amusing scenarios that exemplify the challenges and victories of maintaining quality in the midst of complexity.

Furthermore, this section reminds us that even the most meticulous processes can sometimes go awry by presenting the funniest quality control mishaps. The Quality Jester encourages us to approach quality control with a sense of humour, embracing these imperfect moments and learning from them.

To cope with the often-accompanying stress of quality management, the toolbox of the Quality Jester includes humorous techniques to reduce stress. From witty one-liners to entertaining exercises, this section provides practical strategies to infuse laughter into daily quality control activities, promoting a healthier and more enjoyable work environment.

In summary, the Quality Jester brings a comedic approach to quality control, highlighting the power of laughter and its ability to enhance problem-solving, boost morale, and reduce stress. Quality managers who embrace the qualities of the Quality Jester can guide their roles with a carefree perspective that fosters creativity, camaraderie, and success in the pursuit of quality excellence.

Once upon a time, in the realm of quality control, there was a diligent quality manager named Adam. Adam was known for his thoroughness and meticulous attention to detail. His colleagues often admired his ability to spot even the tiniest defects in products or processes. However, there was one particular incident that showcased Adam's unique approach to quality control.

One day, the company received a batch of faulty products from a supplier. The defects were subtle and difficult to detect, causing frustration among the quality team. As they struggled to identify the root cause, Adam stepped in with a mischievous glimmer in his eyes.

Instead of diving headfirst into the complex analysis, Adam decided to take a light-hearted approach. He gathered the team and announced, "Ladies and gentlemen, today we embark on a quest to unveil the mystery of the invisible gremlin that has invaded our products! But fear not, for I have devised a whimsical plan to capture this elusive creature."

This was a strange attitude for the team in the beginning. They were stunned, but still, this unexpected exit caught the attention of the team. With the team's curiosity piqued, Adam transformed the quality control process into a playful investigation. He distributed magnifying glasses, colourful hats, and detective badges to everyone, turning the lab into a stage for their comedic performance.

Adam assigned humorous code names to each team member, such as "The Defect Detective," "The Quality Inspector Extraordinaire," and "The Guardian of Specifications." They comically role-played their characters, examining the products with exaggerated seriousness while exchanging witty banter and playful accusations.

As the investigation unfolded, Adam encouraged everyone to share their wildest theories and outlandish explanations for the defects. The atmosphere in the lab was filled with laughter and camaraderie, creating an environment where creativity thrived.

During one particularly hilarious moment, Adam picked up a faulty product and pretended to interrogate it. He put on a deep voice and asked, "Tell me, dear product, who let you out of the factory with such a sly defect? Was it the mischievous gremlin or the clumsy fairy?" The team burst into laughter, momentarily forgetting the frustration of the situation.

As the laughter subsided, the team's mindset began to shift. They approached the problem with renewed energy, thinking outside the box and exploring unconventional angles. Through their humorous exploration, they discovered an overlooked step in the production process that was causing the defects.

Adam's comedic approach to quality control not only lifted the team's spirits but also sparked their creativity. By infusing humour into their work, they were able to uncover solutions that might have otherwise remained hidden. The incident became a defining moment in the team's journey, demonstrating the power of laughter in problem-solving.

From that day forward, Adam became known as the Quality Jester, a champion of comedic innovation in quality control. His unique approach inspired others to embrace a light-hearted perspective and find joy in their pursuit of excellence.

The story of Adam, the Quality Jester, serves as a reminder that humour can be a valuable tool in quality control. By injecting laughter into the process, teams can foster a positive and creative work environment, where innovative solutions thrive. Adam's story highlights the importance of finding joy in the journey and the transformative power of a comedic approach to quality control.

It was a bright Monday morning at the bustling headquarters of GomuGomu Manufacturing. Adam, with his signature bowtie and mischievous smile, stepped into the office ready to tackle the day's quality control tasks. In the fast-paced world of quality management, where countless documents and procedures are essential for maintaining high standards, Adam found himself facing a challenge that would put his comedic talents to the test. It all began one fateful day when the company announced a major overhaul of its document management system.

As the designated quality manager responsible for ensuring the smooth transition, Adam eagerly embraced the task. Armed with his trusty magnifying glass and a stack of documents, he dove headfirst into the world of version control, revisions, and countless acronyms.

Days turned into weeks, and weeks into months as Adam tirelessly worked to implement the new document management system. However, despite his best efforts, chaos seemed to follow in his wake. Documents went missing, versions clashed, and confusion reigned supreme.

In the midst of the document management mayhem, Adam found himself in a precarious situation. During a crucial meeting, he accidentally handed out the wrong document to the entire team—a document filled with whimsical doodles and amusing one-liners. Gasps filled the room as the team members glanced at each other, trying to suppress their laughter.

Adam, never one to shy away from an opportunity to entertain, quickly recovered from the embarrassment. With a mischievous grin, he declared, "Ladies and gentlemen, it seems that we have discovered the elusive 'Quality Comic' edition of our document! It's a secret treasure, designed to inject some much-needed humour into our quality management journey."

Laughter erupted throughout the room as the tension dissipated. Adam's ability to find humour even in the face of document management mishaps brought a sense of camaraderie and lightness to the team. Rather than dwelling on the mistakes, they saw the value of a momentary escape from the seriousness of their work.

As the project progressed, Adam recognized that while structure and precision were crucial, a touch of levity could help alleviate the stress associated with document management. He implemented quirky naming conventions for file versions, adorned bulletin boards with humorous quality-related cartoons, and even organized impromptu "document discovery" games to encourage colleagues to explore and engage with the new system.

Adam's approach not only improved the efficiency of the document management process but also fostered a positive and collaborative work environment. Team members embraced the notion that quality management didn't have to be dry and monotonous. They discovered that incorporating humour and light-heartedness into their day-to-day activities enhanced creativity, reduced stress, and strengthened their dedication to maintaining high-quality standards.

18

In the end, the document management overhaul proved to be a success, thanks in no small part to Adam's comedic approach. As the company moved forward with their improved system, the memories of the "Quality Comic" document and the laughter it brought remained etched in the team's minds.

And so, dear readers, let Adam's story serve as a reminder that even in the world of quality control and document management, a dash of humour can go a long way. Embrace the unexpected, find joy in the occasional mishaps, and let laughter be your guiding force. Adam, the Quality Jester, has shown us that by infusing light-heartedness into our work, we can create a more vibrant and productive quality management experience.

Our journey in quality management revolves around tackling various challenges and managing risks, which often leads us to work under constant stress and tension. It is in this context that we met Adam, who challenges the notion of normalizing the intense nature of our work. I don't mean to refer to him as just Adam. Instead, I want you to reflect on how you perceive him at this stage. Are you frustrated with Adam's approach in these two stories, or are you open to learning from him?

Individuals with a penchant for humour in serious work environments can sometimes be seen as disruptive or not taking their job seriously enough. However, when it comes to quality, the humour we incorporate into our sense of responsibility can be used as a tool to invite everyone towards a common goal.

In our early years of school, we used to laugh when a friend made a mistake. Over time, as this behaviour was deemed unacceptable, we began to lose our sense of humour when faced with errors. However, as we grew older, we were taught that when you fall, you should laugh at yourself first. Falling could be both painful and funny at the same time. It's time to apply a similar perspective to quality management.

Things that pose a threat to life are not humorous. However, injecting a bit of joy into process management, thus blending education with humour, can lead to effective and lasting development. Adding some light-heartedness to the hiccups in our quality management journey harms no one. In fact, it opens up new avenues for growth and fosters a more engaging and enjoyable environment.

So, dear readers, as we wrap up this chapter, take a moment to ponder: Are you willing to embrace Adam's unconventional approach and discover the power of humour in quality management? Remember, our work is serious, but that doesn't mean we can't find moments of levity along the way. Laughter has the ability to transform the way we perceive challenges and create a positive, resilient, and collaborative atmosphere. Let us embark on this journey with open minds and hearts, ready to explore the transformative impact of the Quality Jester's comedic approach to quality control.

Chapter 3: Hilarious Anecdotes from the Quality Management Trenches

In the world of quality management, where meticulous attention to detail and adherence to standards are paramount, there lies a treasure trove of hilarious anecdotes. These stories, often shared in hushed whispers among quality professionals, reveal the lighter side of an otherwise serious field. They provide a unique perspective on how humour and innovation can intertwine to create a pathway towards a more innovative approach to quality management.

In the world of quality management, inspections are an essential part of ensuring adherence to standards and identifying potential issues. However, even the most meticulously planned inspections can take unexpected turns, leading to hilarious and memorable moments.

One such incident occurred during an inspection at a manufacturing plant. Eva, a resourceful and mischievous quality manager, was leading the team through the production line when they stumbled upon a peculiar sight–a rubber chicken nestled among the machinery. Confusion and amusement spread among the team members as they tried to comprehend how a rubber chicken found its way into a serious industrial setting.

Eva, known for her innovative thinking, immediately saw an opportunity to turn this unexpected surprise into something beneficial. She picked up the rubber chicken and declared, "Ladies and gentlemen, behold our newest addition to the quality management team–the Rubber

Chicken Quality Assistant! It's here to bring a dose of humour and innovation to our inspections!"

The team erupted in laughter, intrigued by Eva's unorthodox approach. Little did they know that Eva had a mischievous plan up her sleeve. She decided to take the rubber chicken antics to the next level by incorporating it as an AI-modified tool for the quality management system.

Eva, with the help of a tech-savvy team member, programmed the rubber chicken to emit reminders and notifications for different perspectives of quality management. The chicken would cluck and squawk at specific intervals, catching the team's attention and reminding them of crucial quality control practices.

During inspections, as the team diligently worked through their checklist, the rubber chicken would periodically come to life, emitting quirky sounds and reminders. For example, it would cluck to remind them of the importance of precision in measurements or squawk to emphasize the significance of communication between departments.

24

The chicken's presence became both amusing and practical. It not only brought smiles to the team's faces but also served as a unique way to reinforce key quality management principles. The team affectionately referred to it as their "Feathered Quality Guru."

As word spread throughout the plant about the innovative rubber chicken, other departments became intrigued by its potential. They started requesting visits from the Rubber Chicken Quality Assistant, hoping to experience its humorous reminders and gain a fresh perspective on quality management.

Eva, always eager to embrace new ideas, saw an opportunity to further enhance the chicken's capabilities. She collaborated with the plant's IT department to develop a mobile application that would sync with the rubber chicken. This app allowed employees to receive quality management reminders and notifications directly to their smartphones, creating a seamless integration between technology and the amusing rubber chicken.

The chicken became a sensation within the company, with employees eagerly anticipating its clucks and squawks. It became a symbol of the plant's commitment to fostering a positive and innovative work environment. The plant even created a mascot costume of a giant rubber chicken, which Eva wore during quality management training sessions, spreading laughter and knowledge simultaneously.

In the end, what started as a simple rubber chicken among the machinery became an integral part of the plant's quality management system. The chicken's comedic presence reminded everyone that even in the most serious of tasks, humour and innovation could coexist.

As the plant continued to improve its quality management practices, the rubber chicken served as a constant reminder of the importance of different perspectives and creative thinking. Eva's inventive use of the rubber chicken not only brought joy and laughter but also contributed to a culture of continuous improvement and excellence.

And so, dear readers, let Eva's story inspire you to embrace unexpected surprises and think outside the box in your quality management endeavours. Remember, even a rubber chicken can serve as a catalyst for innovative ideas and improvements, reminding us that a little laughter goes a long way in creating a vibrant and productive workplace.

Audits are known for their meticulous scrutiny and detailed examination of processes. However, amidst the seriousness of audits, there are moments of unexpected quirkiness and encounters that leave a lasting impression.

At Makbul Family Corporation, during a particularly rigorous audit, the quality team found themselves face-to-face with an auditor named Sarah, who had an uncanny resemblance to a well-known fictional character. With her distinctive round glasses and lightning-shaped scar, it was hard not to draw parallels to a certain famous wizard.

As the audit progressed, Adam couldn't help but notice the striking resemblance and the opportunity for a touch of whimsy. During a brief break, he approached Sarah and with a twinkle in his eye, said, "You know, Sarah, you bear a striking resemblance to a certain famous wizard. Shall we cast a spell to ensure quality excellence?" Sarah, amused by the comparison, played along and responded with a witty retort, igniting a playful banter between them.

The rest of the team caught wind of the exchange and couldn't help but join in, comparing themselves to other beloved characters from the wizarding world. The serious atmosphere transformed into one filled with laughter and camaraderie. What could have been a tense and stressful audit became an unexpected bonding experience between the auditors and the quality team.

The light-heartedness continued throughout the audit, with references to spells and magical creatures popping up in discussions. The shared laughter and light-hearted moments not only strengthened the relationship between the auditors and the quality team but also facilitated open communication and collaboration. It showcased the power of humour in breaking down barriers and creating a positive audit experience.

As the audit progressed, Sarah, the auditor with her wizard-like resemblance, embraced the playful atmosphere created by the quality team. She began incorporating wizarding references into her audit reports, using phrases like "mischief managed" to signify areas of improvement and "exceeding expectations like a Firebolt broomstick" for commendable processes.

One memorable day during the audit, the team discovered a minor deviation in a critical control point. Instead of the usual serious discussion and corrective action plans, Sarah conjured up a metaphorical scenario. She compared the control point deviation to a rogue Niffler, a mischievous creature known for its obsession with shiny objects. With a mischievous grin, Sarah said, "Looks like we have a Niffler situation here! Let's chase away those shiny distractions and get back on track!"

Inspired by Sarah's whimsical approach, the quality team played along and joined in the metaphorical adventure. They imagined themselves as wizarding inspectors, armed with wands (in this case, their trusty clipboards), hunting down the mischievous Niffler and restoring order to the control point. Laughter echoed through the audit room as they engaged in this imaginative exercise.

Throughout the audit, the team discovered that Sarah's playful nature did not undermine her professionalism or attention to detail. In fact, it enhanced the audit process by fostering a relaxed and collaborative environment. Sarah's ability to combine thoroughness with humour allowed the team to view the audit as an opportunity for growth rather than a mere assessment.

By the end of the audit, the quality team and Sarah had forged a unique bond. The auditors had become more than just scrutinizers of processes; they had become allies in the pursuit of quality excellence. Sarah's approach had not only made the audit experience enjoyable but had also left a lasting impact on the team's perspective of audits.

From that day forward, whenever auditors from Makbul Family Corporation returned for subsequent audits, they were greeted with excitement and anticipation. The team eagerly looked forward to the quirky encounters and the shared laughter that would ensue. Sarah had inadvertently shown them that audits could be more than just compliance exercises—they could be opportunities for innovation, growth, and a little bit of magic.

The quirky side of audits had not only lightened the mood but had also inspired the team to view auditors as valuable allies in their continuous improvement journey.

Sarah had unknowingly become a catalyst for a shift in perspective, proving that a touch of humour and imagination could enhance the effectiveness of audits and create a positive and collaborative environment.

And so, dear readers, let this tale remind you that audits need not be dry and burdensome. Embrace the quirkiness, find joy in the unexpected encounters, and let humour be your guide. Like Sarah, the auditors who embrace the playful side of audits can foster an environment of trust, creativity, and innovation in the realm of quality management.

Mistakes are an inevitable part of any quality management process. However, rather than dwelling on the errors, embracing a light-hearted perspective can turn these blunders into moments of laughter and learning.

In one memorable incident at the bustling headquarters of No Way to Home Manufacturing, a company known for its commitment to excellence despite its unconventional name, the quality team found themselves facing an unexpected challenge. Ethan, a diligent team member with a knack for comedic mishaps, accidentally knocked over a tray of freshly baked cookies onto a stack of important documents. The room filled with gasps and sighs of frustration as the team witnessed the unfortunate collision of confectionery and paperwork.

However, amidst the collective disappointment, Finn, a quick-witted and light-hearted quality manager, saw an opportunity for laughter. He rushed to Ethan's side and, with a mischievous grin, grabbed a cookie covered in ink smudges. With a theatrical flourish, Finn held it up like a trophy and declared, "Behold, the birth of the 'Cookie Crunch' edition—a delicious blend of quality management and dessert delights!"

The room erupted with laughter as Finn took a bite of the cookie, pretending to savour its unique flavour. His playful act instantly diffused the tension and turned the incident into a moment of shared amusement. Ethan, though initially mortified, couldn't help but join in the laughter, realizing that mistakes could be catalysts for unexpected moments of joy.

In that moment, the team's perspective shifted. Instead of dwelling on the mishap, they embraced Finn's light-hearted approach and redirected their focus to finding creative solutions and preventive measures for similar incidents. Amidst the laughter, they brainstormed ideas, their camaraderie growing stronger with each shared joke.

From that day forward, the "Cookie Crunch" incident became a symbol of embracing mistakes and finding humour in the face of adversity at No Way to Home

Manufacturing. Whenever a blunder occurred, the team would fondly recall Finn's triumphant pose with the ink-stained cookie, and it served as a reminder to approach challenges with resilience and a positive mindset.

The incident had a profound effect on the team's culture. They began to view mistakes as opportunities for growth and innovation, recognizing that even in the face of setbacks, they could find a way to laugh and learn. The spirit of camaraderie and a light-hearted approach permeated their work, fostering an environment of creativity and continuous improvement.

These hilarious anecdotes from the quality management trenches remind us that laughter and a positive perspective can coexist with rigorous quality control. By embracing the unexpected, finding humour in blunders, and laughing at mistakes, we create a pathway to innovation and a more enjoyable quality management journey. The "Cookie Crunch" incident at No Way to Home Manufacturing served as a reminder that even in the most unexpected moments, there is always room for laughter and growth.

KEY Learnings from chapter 2:

The stories in this chapter highlight the importance of infusing humour, embracing unconventional approaches, and fostering a positive work culture within the context of audits and quality management. By incorporating light-heartedness, auditors and quality professionals can:

1. Create a positive and collaborative audit experience: Embracing humour and playful banter during audits can break down barriers, foster open communication, and strengthen relationships between auditors and the quality team. Laughter and camaraderie help create a positive audit experience that facilitates collaboration and constructive feedback.

2. Stimulate creativity and innovation: Introducing whimsical elements and unexpected perspectives into the audit process can stimulate creativity and innovation. By thinking outside the box, auditors and quality professionals can uncover new insights, identify improvement opportunities, and

explore unconventional solutions to quality challenges.

3. Foster a resilient and adaptable work environment: Finding humour in mistakes and unexpected situations allows teams to develop resilience and adaptability. Rather than dwelling on blunders or mishaps, embracing a light-hearted perspective encourages teams to learn from mistakes, find innovative solutions, and maintain a positive attitude in the face of challenges.

4. Enhance engagement and motivation: Incorporating humour and unconventional approaches into the audit process increases engagement and motivation among auditors and the quality team. By creating a fun and enjoyable work environment, individuals are more likely to be enthusiastic, proactive, and committed to achieving high-quality standards.

Breaking the ice and building rapport: The use of humour in audits can help break the ice and create a more relaxed and comfortable environment. It allows auditors and the quality team to build rapport, establish a connection, and foster a sense of camaraderie. This can lead to better communication, collaboration, and a more productive audit process.

Humanizing the audit process: Audits are often seen as formal and intimidating processes. However, incorporating humour humanizes the audit experience. It reminds everyone involved that auditors are not just inspectors, but individuals with a sense of humour and a shared goal of improving quality. This human element fosters a more positive and empathetic audit environment.

Encouraging risk-taking and learning from mistakes: By laughing at mistakes and blunders, the stories in this chapter highlight the importance of embracing a culture of learning. Auditors and the quality team are encouraged to take risks, try new approaches, and learn from their failures. This mindset promotes a continuous improvement mindset and an organizational culture that values innovation and growth.

Finding joy in the process: Quality management can sometimes be perceived as a serious and monotonous endeavour. The anecdotes in this chapter remind us to find joy and enjoyment in the process. By infusing humour, creativity, and playfulness into the audit and quality management journey, individuals can maintain enthusiasm, passion, and a sense of fulfilment in their work.

Overall, the stories in Chapter 2 emphasize the importance of embracing humour, humanizing the audit process, fostering a culture of learning, and finding joy in quality management. By doing so, auditors and quality professionals can create a more engaging, innovative, and enjoyable work environment while achieving the highest standards of quality excellence.

Chapter 4: Laughing Through Quality Improvement

In the intricate realm of quality management, where precision and adherence to standards reign supreme, an unconventional ally awaits in the wings — laughter. Beyond its role as a simple expression of joy, laughter possesses the remarkable power to transform the very fabric of quality control. It defies convention, turning missteps into stepping stones, auditors from critics into companions, and challenges into gateways of innovation. This chapter unveils the potent influence of laughter as a tool within the quality management arsenal. As we journey through stories and insights, we discover how humor breathes life into the rigorous pursuit of quality excellence, reshaping mindsets, enlivening processes, and fostering a work culture that thrives on both precision and positivity. Join us as we explore the uncharted territories where laughter and quality management intertwine, revealing an unforeseen synergy that elevates both practice and people."

At "Laughalot Co.," a company renowned for its vibrant and light-hearted culture, the quality team faced a perplexing challenge in their production line. They were struggling to meet the stringent quality standards for their signature product, the Giggle Widget. Despite their best efforts, traditional problem-solving methods seemed to fall short.

The issue plaguing the production line was an inconsistent alignment of the Giggle Widget's components, resulting in frequent quality defects and customer dissatisfaction. The team had tried various corrective measures, but the root cause of the misalignment remained elusive.

Enter Emily, a team member known for her quick wit and out-of-the-box thinking. Recognizing the power of comedy to spark creativity, she proposed an unconventional approach to finding solutions—the "Humour Hackathon."

During the Humour Hackathon, team members gathered in a room filled with laughter and playful energy. They unleashed their comedic talents, brainstorming hilarious and seemingly absurd ideas to improve the quality of the Giggle Widget. From using clown shoes as production equipment to incorporating whoopee cushions for quality testing, the ideas flowed freely, and laughter filled the air.

Although many of the ideas were outrageous, they served as catalysts for innovative thinking. Amidst the humour, a few ideas emerged that held promise. Inspired by the idea of incorporating laughter into the production process, the team experimented with sound vibrations and implemented a "Giggle Generator" that emitted joyful noises during the widget assembly.

To their surprise, this unconventional approach had a positive impact on the quality of the Giggle Widget. The light-hearted atmosphere and the infusion of humour into the production line not only boosted team morale but also led to creative problem-solving and improved quality outcomes.

The team discovered that the misalignment issue was partly caused by the lack of synchronized movements during the assembly process. The Giggle Generator, with its joyful vibrations, served as a fun and effective solution to address this root cause. The synchronized vibrations helped align the components accurately, reducing defects and ensuring consistent quality in the Giggle Widget.

As a preventive measure, Laughalot Co. implemented a "Laughter Reminder System" throughout the production line. This innovative system used AI-powered tools to emit periodic bursts of laughter, reminding the operators to maintain a playful mindset and be attentive to quality standards. The system not only provided a light-hearted atmosphere but also acted as a gentle nudge to prevent complacency and maintain focus on quality improvement.

Laughalot Co. learned a valuable lesson through this experience: comedy and creativity can lead to unconventional solutions. By embracing humour and encouraging out-of-the-box thinking, they were able to break free from conventional constraints and discover innovative approaches to quality improvement. The Humour Hackathon became a regular event at the company, fostering a culture of laughter, collaboration, and continuous improvement.

In this whimsical journey of quality management, Laughalot Co. demonstrated that a hearty laugh and a playful mindset can pave the way to ground-breaking solutions, making the pursuit of quality improvement an enjoyable and rewarding endeavour.

At Naruto Pharmaceutical Solutions, a company dedicated to enhancing human well-being through innovative healthcare solutions, the quality team embarked on a journey of continuous improvement. They were determined to optimize their packaging process for their range of medical supplies and ensure that each product reached customers in perfect condition.

However, a persistent challenge haunted the packaging line—occasional mix-ups in labelling, leading to incorrect product identification. The team realized that a mislabelled product could have serious consequences, compromising patient safety and undermining the company's reputation. They needed to address this issue promptly and effectively.

Recognizing the power of a playful perspective in problem-solving, the team decided to infuse fun into their continuous improvement efforts. They transformed their improvement meetings into "Innovation Fiesta" sessions, where creativity and laughter were encouraged.

During one such Innovation Fiesta, Juanita, a team member with a knack for humour, shared a comical story about her experience as a child, mistaking a bottle of cough syrup for a soda. The room erupted in laughter, and this shared moment of amusement sparked a lively discussion on how to prevent labelling mix-ups.

Through their collaborative efforts, the team identified the root cause of the problem—a lack of clear visual cues during the packaging process. They realized that the similarity in design and colour of the labels contributed to the mix-ups. To address this, they implemented corrective actions, including redesigning the labels with distinct colours and introducing prominent product images that were hard to mistake.

To prevent future mix-ups, the team came up with a brilliant idea—they decided to incorporate a playful element into the packaging process. They developed a "Label Shuffle Dance," where operators performed a lively dance routine as they affixed the labels onto the products. This engaging activity not only added an element of fun to the work environment but also served as a visual cue for the correct labelling process.

Furthermore, Naruto Pharmaceutical Solutions implemented a "Quality Check Playlist" as a preventive measure. The operators were encouraged to listen to upbeat music while conducting quality checks. The catchy tunes not only elevated their mood but also helped maintain focus and attention to detail, reducing the likelihood of labelling errors.

By infusing a playful perspective into their continuous improvement efforts, Naruto Pharmaceutical Solutions successfully addressed the labelling mix-up issue. The combination of distinct labels, the Label Shuffle Dance, and the Quality Check Playlist contributed to a significant reduction in errors, ensuring that the right products reached the right customers.

This light-hearted approach to continuous improvement fostered a culture of creativity and joy within the company. The Innovation Fiesta became a recurring event, where team members eagerly shared their funny anecdotes, innovative ideas, and successes. The playful perspective not only improved the packaging process but also enhanced team collaboration, morale, and pride in their work.

Naruto Pharmaceutical Solutions learned that embracing a playful perspective can unlock new dimensions of continuous improvement. By infusing fun, humour, and creative approaches into their quality management practices, they were able to drive positive change, strengthen their commitment to excellence, and deliver safe and reliable healthcare solutions to their customers.

In this vibrant journey of continuous improvement, Naruto Pharmaceutical Solutions demonstrated that a playful perspective can be a catalyst for innovation, transforming the pursuit of quality excellence into an enjoyable and fulfilling endeavour.

At PembeliBukle Tech Solutions, a company specializing in cutting-edge technology solutions, the quality team embarked on a mission to optimize their software development process. They aimed to streamline their workflow, reduce bottlenecks, and enhance overall efficiency.

Harika, an enthusiastic and creative team member, recognized the potential for humour to bring a fresh perspective to the process optimization journey. She believed that injecting laughter into the often-intense atmosphere of process improvement meetings could foster creativity and collaboration among the team.

During a brainstorming session focused on identifying bottlenecks, Harika shared a hilarious story from her college days. She vividly described an incident when she attempted to write code while battling a pesky fly in her room. The entire team burst into laughter as they imagined her frantic attempts to swat the fly while trying to maintain focus on her coding task.

Inspired by Harika's story, the team decided to approach process optimization with a light-hearted mindset. They transformed their improvement meetings into "Optimization Comedy Hour," where each team member shared funny anecdotes and jokes related to their experiences in software development.

As they delved into the optimization process, the team identified a root cause of their bottlenecks—a lack of effective communication and collaboration between different departments. Siloed information and delays in sharing updates often led to confusion, rework, and missed deadlines.

To address this issue, the team implemented a corrective action plan. They introduced a digital platform called "JesterConnect" to facilitate seamless communication and real-time collaboration. JesterConnect provided a playful and user-friendly interface, encouraging team members to share updates, ask questions, and provide feedback in an engaging and enjoyable manner.

As a preventive measure, PembeliBukle Tech Solutions implemented a practice called "Laughter Breaks." At regular intervals during the workday, team members were encouraged to take short breaks and engage in fun activities such as sharing funny memes, telling jokes, or participating in team-building games. These laughter breaks served as stress relievers, fostering a positive work environment and boosting team morale.

With the introduction of humour and the implementation of JesterConnect and laughter breaks, PembeliBukle Tech Solutions witnessed a remarkable transformation in their software development process. Effective communication improved, collaboration thrived, and the team's collective creativity flourished.

The Optimization Comedy Hour became a cherished tradition within the company, providing a platform for team members to share funny stories, lighten the mood, and build stronger bonds. Laughter and humour became integral to their process optimization journey, reminding everyone that work can be enjoyable while striving for excellence.

Through their commitment to finding humour in process optimization, PembeliBukle Tech Solutions not only improved their workflow and productivity but also nurtured a vibrant and inclusive company culture. The light-hearted approach led to enhanced creativity, strengthened team dynamics, and a shared sense of purpose.

In the quest for process optimization, PembeliBukle Tech Solutions discovered that humour can be a powerful tool. By lightening the load and finding joy in the journey, they transformed the process optimization journey into an exciting and rewarding adventure, setting the stage for continuous growth and success.

In this chapter, we explored the power of humour and a playful perspective in the realm of quality improvement. Each story highlighted different aspects of how laughter and light-heartedness can positively impact the quality management process. Here are some key lessons we can take away from Chapter 4:

1. Unconventional Solutions: Comedy and Creativity

- Embracing humour and unconventional thinking can spark creativity and lead to innovative solutions.

- Thinking beyond traditional constraints allows us to explore new possibilities and break through barriers.

- Laughter and playfulness can help us approach challenges with a fresh perspective and open-mindedness.

2. Fun with Continuous Improvement: A Playful Perspective

- Injecting humour into continuous improvement efforts can foster collaboration and engagement among team members.

- Finding joy in the improvement journey makes the process more enjoyable and encourages active participation.

- By creating a positive and light-hearted atmosphere, teams can work together more effectively and overcome obstacles.

3. Finding Humour in Process Optimization: Lightening the Load

- Integrating humour into process optimization efforts can alleviate stress and create a positive work environment.

- Sharing funny stories and engaging in laughter breaks can boost morale, relieve tension, and strengthen team dynamics.

- By finding joy in the journey, teams can enhance communication, collaboration, and overall productivity.

Overall, Chapter 4 teaches us that laughter and humour have a rightful place in quality improvement. They can inspire creativity, enhance team dynamics, and foster a positive work culture. Embracing a playful perspective allows us to approach challenges with resilience, innovation, and a sense of enjoyment.

Chapter 5: Quality Quotations and Humorous Insights

In the intricate landscape of quality management, where precision and standards stand as the guiding stars, a touch of humour can be the unexpected spark that ignites innovation and camaraderie. In this chapter, we embark on a journey into the worlds of Marvel, anime, comedians, and clever wordplay to explore how these diverse perspectives infuse quality management with a fresh lightness.

In this chapter, we dive into the world of Marvel and explore how famous Marvel characters provide humorous insights on quality management. Through their unique quotes, these characters not only entertain but also offer valuable lessons in creative thinking, team bonding, and communication.

The inclusion of Marvel characters in quality management discussions serves as a creative and engaging way to approach the topic. By drawing parallels between their extraordinary abilities and the challenges of quality management, we can find common ground and foster a sense of shared interest among team members.

The quotes from characters like Hawkeye, Loki, Bruce Banner, Daredevil, Professor X, and Moon Knight highlight the importance of key aspects in quality management:

Creative Thinking: Marvel characters encourage us to think outside the box, embracing unconventional approaches to problem-solving. Their witty quotes remind us that humour and creativity go hand in hand, providing fresh perspectives and sparking innovative ideas.

Team Bonding: The use of Marvel characters creates a sense of camaraderie and bonding within the team. By referencing these well-known figures, team members with shared interests can connect on a different level, strengthening their relationships and fostering a positive work environment.

Communication: Marvel quotes serve as conversation starters, facilitating communication and dialogue among team members. The playful nature of these quotes encourages open discussions, allowing for the exchange of ideas and experiences related to quality management challenges.

By incorporating humour and the world of Marvel into quality management discussions, we promote a light-hearted and enjoyable approach to a sometimes-serious topic. This chapter reminds us of the power of creative thinking, team bonding, and effective communication in driving quality improvement initiatives.

Ultimately, the combination of humour and Marvel characters sparks inspiration and encourages us to approach quality management with a fresh perspective. It highlights the importance of embracing creativity, building strong team connections, and fostering effective communication to achieve excellence in quality management practices.

Marvel characters have captivated audiences with their heroic adventures and witty dialogue. In this section, we explore how these beloved characters offer their humorous insights on quality management. Through their fictional quotes, they shed light on the importance of maintaining high standards and finding humour in the process.

Let's look what marvel characters would say for quality:

Iron Man (Tony Stark): "In the world of quality management, there's no room for 'irony'—only iron-clad standards!"

Iron Man, known for his genius intellect and cutting-edge technology, delivers a witty line that underscores the seriousness of quality management. His play on the word "irony" emphasizes the need for unwavering standards and attention to detail, reminding us that precision is key in achieving optimal quality.

Spider-Man (Peter Parker): "With great quality comes great responsibility—also, a friendly neighbourhood Spider-Quality Inspector wouldn't hurt!"

Spider-Man, the friendly neighbourhood superhero, brings his light-hearted nature to the topic of quality management. By paraphrasing his famous line, "With great power comes great responsibility," he playfully highlights the correlation between quality and responsibility. His humorous suggestion of a "Spider-Quality Inspector" injects a dose of fun into the discussion.

Deadpool (Wade Wilson): "Quality management is like a chimichanga—spicy, unpredictable, and best enjoyed with a sense of humour!"

Deadpool, known for his irreverent humour and unpredictable nature, offers a humorous take on quality management. By likening it to his favourite food, the chimichanga, he captures the spicy and unpredictable nature of maintaining quality standards. Deadpool's quote reminds us to approach quality management with a sense of humour, embracing the challenges and enjoying the process.

Thor: "Quality management is like wielding Mjolnir—it requires strength, precision, and a good sense of humour to deal with Loki-like quality issues!"

Thor, the God of Thunder, draws a parallel between quality management and his mighty hammer, Mjolnir. He highlights the need for strength and precision in ensuring quality but also emphasizes the importance of maintaining a sense of humour when facing unexpected challenges, much like dealing with his mischievous brother Loki.

Black Widow (Natasha Romanoff): "Quality management is a delicate dance—grace, precision, and a quick wit are the key moves!"

Black Widow, known for her agility and strategic thinking, offers a metaphorical insight into quality management. She likens it to a dance, emphasizing the need for grace, precision, and a quick wit to navigate the complexities of maintaining quality. Her quote reminds us that quality management requires both technical expertise and adaptability.

Hawkeye (Clint Barton): "In quality management, accuracy is my bullseye. I never miss the mark!"

Hawkeye, known for his exceptional archery skills and precision, playfully relates his expertise to quality management. By referencing his bullseye accuracy, he emphasizes the importance of accuracy and attention to detail in maintaining quality standards.

Loki: "Quality management can be as unpredictable as my mischief. Embrace the chaos and turn it into controlled excellence!"

Loki, the mischievous and cunning Asgardian, adds his unique perspective to quality management. With his quote, he encourages embracing the unpredictability of the process while finding ways to channel it into controlled excellence, just as he turns chaos into calculated schemes.

Bruce Banner (The Hulk): "Quality management might make me angry, but I always strive for 'incredible' results!"

Bruce Banner, the scientist with a temperamental alter ego, humorously acknowledges the frustrations that can arise in quality management. However, he emphasizes his determination to achieve incredible results despite the challenges, reflecting the importance of perseverance and a positive mindset.

Daredevil (Matt Murdock): "In the world of quality management, my senses are heightened. I can 'hear' the defects and 'sense' the improvements!"

Daredevil, the blind superhero with heightened senses, humorously applies his abilities to quality management. By emphasizing his ability to detect defects and sense improvements, he highlights the importance of keen observation and attention to detail in maintaining quality standards.

Professor X (Charles Xavier): "In quality management, my mind is a telepathic powerhouse. I can 'read' the needs of customers and 'mentally project' continuous improvement!"

Professor X, the powerful telepath and leader of the X-Men, adds a touch of humour to quality management. By referencing his telepathic abilities, he playfully suggests his capacity to understand customer needs and project continuous improvement mentally, showcasing the importance of empathy and strategic thinking.

Moon Knight (Marc Spector): "Quality management is like the phases of the moon—cyclical challenges that require vigilance and a little lunacy!"

Moon Knight, a complex and often enigmatic hero, offers an analogy between quality management and the phases of the moon. By comparing the cyclical nature of quality challenges to the moon's phases, he highlights the need for vigilance and adaptability, with a hint of playful lunacy.

These humorous insights from Marvel characters, including Hawkeye, Loki, Bruce Banner, Daredevil, Professor X, and Moon Knight, showcase their unique perspectives on quality management, adding a touch of fun and imagination to the discussion.

In this chapter, we explore the world of anime and how famous anime characters provide insightful and humorous perspectives on quality management. Anime, known for its unique storytelling and captivating characters, offers valuable lessons that can be applied to quality management practices. By drawing inspiration from these characters, we can gain fresh insights and a new perspective on various aspects of quality management.

Anime characters often possess distinct traits and face challenging situations, making their insights particularly relevant. Let's dive into some examples of how these characters humorously shed light on quality management and what we can learn from them:

Goku from Dragon Ball Z: "Quality management is like mastering the Super Saiyan transformation. It requires continuous training, perseverance, and pushing past your limits to achieve excellence."

Goku's quote emphasizes the importance of continuous improvement and pushing oneself to achieve the highest quality standards. Just as Goku trains tirelessly to unlock new levels of power, quality management requires a commitment to ongoing learning, growth, and surpassing previous achievements.

> **Luffy from One Piece:** "Quality management is like sailing the Grand Line. It's an adventure filled with unexpected challenges and the need to adapt and improvise to ensure the best outcomes."

Luffy's analogy highlights the dynamic nature of quality management. Like sailing through uncharted waters, quality management presents unforeseen challenges that require adaptability and quick thinking. It emphasizes the importance of flexibility and embracing change to navigate the unpredictable journey of maintaining high standards.

> **Naruto from Naruto:** "Quality management is like mastering the Rasengan. It requires focus, precision, and infusing your own chakra of expertise to create a powerful impact."

Naruto's comparison draws attention to the importance of focus and precision in quality management. Just as

Naruto channels his chakra into the Rasengan technique to generate a powerful impact, quality management relies on focused attention to detail, expertise, and the ability to deliver high-quality outcomes that leave a lasting impact.

Light Yagami from Death Note: "Quality management is like the ultimate mind game. It requires strategy, analysis, and the ability to outwit potential quality issues."

Light Yagami's perspective brings a strategic aspect to quality management. He views it as a complex mental challenge that requires careful analysis, planning, and the ability to anticipate and overcome potential quality issues. It highlights the importance of proactive problem-solving and staying one step ahead to maintain quality excellence.

Okabe Rintarou from Steins Gate: "Quality management is like time travel. You need to carefully navigate through different possibilities, make adjustments, and ensure the desired outcome."

Okabe's analogy draws parallels between quality management and the intricacies of time travel. Both require a methodical approach, careful decision-making, and the ability to make adjustments along the way. Quality management, like time travel, involves navigating through different scenarios and taking actions to achieve the desired outcome.

Levi Ackerman from Attack on Titan: "Quality management is like defending humanity against Titans. It demands meticulous attention to detail, swift decision-making, and a relentless pursuit of perfection."

Levi's comparison highlights the critical nature of quality management. Just as Levi defends humanity against Titans with meticulous attention to detail, quality management requires a similar level of precision, quick decision-making, and an unwavering commitment to excellence. It emphasizes the need for thoroughness and the relentless pursuit of perfection in quality control.

Saitama from One Punch Man: "Quality management is like being a superhero. It's about consistently delivering exceptional results with minimal effort, but never underestimating the importance of continuous improvement."

Saitama's quote provides a unique perspective on quality management. While he effortlessly defeats enemies with a single punch, his remark emphasizes the importance of consistently delivering exceptional results. It reminds us not to become complacent and to continually seek ways to improve, even when things appear effortless on the surface.

Yato from Noragami: "Quality management is like being a god. It requires dedication, attention to the smallest details, and the ability to adapt and evolve to meet the needs of those you serve."

Yato's comparison highlights the level of commitment and responsibility required in quality management. Just as gods serve and protect their followers, quality management involves a dedication to meeting the needs of customers and stakeholders. It emphasizes the importance of attention to detail and the ability to adapt and evolve in response to changing requirements.

By exploring the perspectives of famous anime characters such as Goku, Luffy, Naruto, Light Yagami, Okabe Rintarou, Levi Ackerman, Saitama, and Yato, we gain unique insights into quality management practices. Their quotes remind us of the importance of continuous improvement, adaptability, precision, strategic thinking, and a touch of light-heartedness in our quality management endeavours.

The inclusion of anime characters in quality management discussions encourages creative thinking, fosters team bonding, and increases communication based on a common interest. Referencing these iconic characters creates a shared experience and enhances team collaboration. By drawing upon the lessons and inspirations from anime characters, we expand our creative thinking and promote a positive and engaging work environment within the realm of quality management.

From the perspective of famous anime characters on quality management, we can learn several key lessons:

1. Embrace continuous improvement: Characters like Goku, Naruto, and Saitama emphasize the importance of ongoing growth and development. They remind us to constantly strive for improvement, push past our limits, and consistently deliver exceptional results.

2. Adaptability and flexibility: Anime characters such as Luffy and Yato highlight the need to adapt and evolve in the face of challenges. Quality management requires the ability to adjust strategies, navigate unexpected situations, and remain flexible to meet changing requirements.

3. Attention to detail: Levi Ackerman and Light Yagami stress the significance of meticulous attention to detail. Quality management demands a thorough approach, careful analysis, and proactive problem-solving to ensure high standards are maintained.

4. Strategic thinking: Characters like Light Yagami and Okabe Rintarou emphasize the importance of strategic planning and decision-making. Quality

management involves analyzing potential risks, devising effective strategies, and staying ahead of potential issues.

5. Relentless pursuit of perfection: Levi Ackerman and Okabe Rintarou inspire us to pursue perfection in quality management. They highlight the need for a relentless commitment to excellence, never settling for mediocrity, and continually seeking ways to improve.

6. Team collaboration and bonding: The inclusion of anime characters in quality management discussions fosters team collaboration and communication based on a shared interest. Referencing these characters can promote a positive and engaging work environment, strengthening team dynamics and encouraging creative thinking.

Overall, the perspective of famous anime characters on quality management reminds us to approach our work with dedication, creativity, and a sense of adventure. By drawing inspiration from these characters, we can infuse our quality management practices with innovation, resilience, and a touch of light-heartedness.

Inviting Comedians' Perspectives to Inject Humour into

Your Quality Management Activities

In this chapter, we explore the power of incorporating comedians' perspectives into your quality management activities. By infusing humour into the workplace, you can create a positive and engaging environment that fosters innovation, collaboration, and continuous improvement.

Comedians have a unique ability to find laughter in everyday situations, and their insights can be invaluable in lightening the mood and sparking creativity. By inviting their perspectives into your quality management activities, you can introduce a new dimension of humour that encourages team bonding and enhances problem-solving.

Imagine hosting a "Comedy Hour" during team meetings or quality improvement workshops. You can share funny anecdotes, witty one-liners, or even comedic sketches related to quality management. This not only brings laughter to the room but also serves as a reminder that mistakes and challenges are part of the journey.

Comedians' perspectives can also be integrated into training programs and seminars. Including humorous videos, skits, or quotes during presentations can capture the audience's attention and make the learning experience more enjoyable. This approach can effectively communicate important quality management principles while keeping participants engaged and entertained.

Moreover, you can organize comedy-themed team-building activities or "Humour of Sense" competitions where team members come up with quality-related jokes, puns, or funny slogans. This not only encourages creative thinking but also promotes a sense of camaraderie and shared humour among team members.

By incorporating comedians' perspectives, you introduce a light-hearted atmosphere that reduces stress, boosts morale, and encourages out-of-the-box thinking. The humour acts as a catalyst for team collaboration, as it breaks down barriers and encourages open communication. It also creates a positive work culture that embraces mistakes as opportunities for growth and welcomes fresh ideas.

Remember, the goal is not to trivialize the importance of quality management but to infuse it with a playful perspective that inspires innovation and continuous improvement. By inviting comedians' perspectives into your quality management activities, you create an environment where laughter and excellence go hand in hand, leading to a more enjoyable and effective quality management journey.

Here are five examples of how you can incorporate comedians' perspectives into your quality management activities:

1. Comedy Hour: Dedicate a portion of your team meetings or quality improvement workshops to a "Comedy Hour." Share funny anecdotes, jokes, or humorous stories related to quality management. This lightens the mood, encourages laughter, and creates a positive and engaging atmosphere for discussion.

2. Humorous Training Materials: Include comedic videos, skits, or quotes in your training programs and seminars. These can be used to introduce

important quality management concepts in a light-hearted and memorable way. Humour captures participants' attention, enhances learning retention, and makes the training experience more enjoyable.

3. Quality Joke Competitions: Organize "Humour of Sense" competitions where team members come up with quality-related jokes, puns, or funny slogans. Encourage everyone to showcase their creativity and wit. This activity fosters team bonding, stimulates innovative thinking, and promotes a shared sense of humour within the team.

4. Comedic Team-Building Activities: Plan team-building activities with a comedy twist. For example, you can organize improvisation exercises, where team members engage in humorous role-playing scenarios related to quality management. These activities promote collaboration, enhance communication skills, and create a fun and inclusive team environment.

5. Comedy-based Brainstorming Sessions: Incorporate comedy into your brainstorming sessions for problem-solving and process improvement. Encourage team members to think creatively and generate funny and unconventional ideas. The humour acts as a catalyst for innovative thinking, breaks down mental barriers, and inspires fresh approaches to quality challenges.

By implementing these examples, you infuse your quality management activities with humour and creativity. This not only reduces stress and increases team morale but also enhances collaboration, communication, and problem-solving capabilities. The incorporation of comedians' perspectives brings a refreshing and light-hearted atmosphere to your quality management initiatives, driving continuous improvement and fostering an enjoyable workplace culture.

In the realm of quality management, humour can serve as a powerful tool to alleviate stress, foster understanding, and create a sense of relatability. Comedians, with their unique ability to find humour in difficult situations, offer valuable insights that can be applied to quality management practices. In this chapter, we explore real quotes from comedians that touch on difficulties, understanding, reducing stress, and being relatable. These quotes remind us of the importance of laughter in navigating challenges and approaching quality management with a light-hearted perspective. Let's delve into the witty and insightful world of comedians and discover how their perspectives can enhance our quality management journey.

1. "Laughter is the shortest distance between two people." - Victor Borge This quote from Victor Borge emphasizes the power of laughter in bridging gaps between individuals and fostering understanding. It highlights how humour can create a shared connection and break down barriers.

2. "You have to laugh at the things that hurt you just to keep yourself in balance, just to keep the world from running you plumb crazy." - Ken Kesey Ken Kesey's quote emphasizes the therapeutic nature of laughter. It suggests that humour can help us

cope with difficult situations, maintain our sanity, and find balance amidst life's challenges.

3. "Comedy is simply a funny way of being serious." - Peter Ustinov This quote from Peter Ustinov reminds us that comedy can be a powerful tool for addressing serious topics. It highlights how humour allows us to approach difficult subjects with a lighter touch, making them more relatable and accessible.

4. "Humour is just another defence against the universe." - Mel Brooks Mel Brooks' quote reflects the idea that humour serves as a defence mechanism against the challenges and uncertainties of life. It implies that finding humour in difficult situations can help us navigate and cope with the complexities of the world.

5. "I think the next best thing to solving a problem is finding some humour in it." - Frank Howard Clark Frank Howard Clark's quote emphasizes the importance of finding humour in problem-solving. It suggests that laughter can provide a fresh

perspective, alleviate stress, and open our minds to innovative solutions.

These quotes from renowned comedians highlight the role of humour in addressing difficulties, fostering understanding, reducing stress, and creating relatability. They underscore the power of laughter in bringing people together, finding balance, and navigating the challenges of life with a lighter heart.

In the world of quality management, a little humour can go a long way. The quotes from comedians we explored in this chapter have shown us the power of laughter in addressing difficulties, fostering understanding, reducing stress, and creating relatability. By embracing humour, we can approach quality management activities with a renewed sense of creativity, resilience, and camaraderie. So, let's invite comedians' perspectives into our sense of humour and infuse our quality management practices with laughter, finding joy in the process and creating a positive and engaging work environment. Remember, when faced with challenges, a good laugh can be the key to unlocking innovative solutions and building stronger teams.

Laughter is a universal language that has the power to bring people together and lighten even the most serious of topics. In the realm of quality management, where precision and standards reign supreme, injecting some humour can add a refreshing twist. Witty one-liners and quality-related puns provide a playful and creative perspective on the intricacies of maintaining high standards. In this section, we explore a collection of humorous quips that offer a light-hearted take on quality management. So, sit back, relax, and prepare for a delightful journey through the world of witty wordplay.

You can also consider these puns and one-liners as a starting point for your own innovative thinking in quality management. As Nur Simsir once said, "Innovation for quality" is the motto, and any idea begins with a starting point. Use these examples as inspiration to build your own adaptive ideas and approaches.

1. "Don't be afraid to 'Excel' in quality management. Just don't make it 'Spreadsheet'!" This pun cleverly combines the popular software "Excel" with the

term "spreadsheet" to highlight the importance of excelling in quality management without getting lost in excessive paperwork. It encourages us to focus on achieving excellence without drowning in administrative tasks.

2. "Quality management is like a 'CAPA'ccino–fix the issues and add a sprinkle of creativity!" This playful pun combines the term "CAPA" (Corrective and Preventive Action) with the popular coffee beverage "cappuccino." It reminds us that addressing issues in quality management requires both corrective actions and a dash of creativity to prevent their recurrence, just like the perfect blend of coffee and foam in a cappuccino.

3. "When it comes to quality management, 'E.T.' doesn't mean 'Extra Terrestrial,' but rather 'Extra Thorough'!" This humorous twist on the acronym "E.T." brings a fresh perspective to quality management. It suggests that in the world of quality, "E.T." represents being extra thorough rather than referring to extra-terrestrial beings. It emphasizes the importance of attention to detail

and going above and beyond in our quality practices.

4. "In the realm of quality management, 'Resistance' is futile—unless it's against non-compliant products!" This clever wordplay combines the concept of resistance in quality management with the iconic phrase from the Star Trek series, "Resistance is futile." It reminds us that while resistance to change can hinder progress, resistance against non-compliant products is essential to maintaining high standards and ensuring quality.

5. "When life gives you 'lemons,' make sure they meet the ISO 9001 lemonade standards!" This pun playfully connects the common saying "When life gives you lemons" with the ISO 9001 quality standard. It encourages us to make the best out of challenging situations and highlights the importance of ensuring even the humblest of ingredients, like lemons, meet the rigorous standards set by quality management systems.

In the world of quality management, a well-placed pun or a clever one-liner can bring a smile to our faces and add a dose of levity to our daily practices. The witty one-liners and quality-related puns we explored in this section remind us that while quality management is a serious undertaking, there's always room for humour and creativity. By incorporating these playful quips into our discussions, we can foster a more engaging and enjoyable environment, enhance team bonding, and spark innovative thinking. So, let's embrace the power of a well-crafted pun, a clever wordplay, and infuse our quality management activities with laughter and wit. Remember, a little humour can go a long way in making our quality journey a delightful and memorable one.

Chapter 6: Hilarious Illustrations: Visualizing Quality Management Funnies

Laughter knows no boundaries, and when it comes to quality management, clever and humorous illustrations can bring a whole new level of enjoyment. In this chapter, we dive into the world of hilarious illustrations that vividly depict the quirks and challenges of quality management. These visual representations not only entertain but also provide valuable insights and relatable moments that resonate with professionals in the field. Get ready to chuckle as we explore a collection of amusing illustrations that shed light on the lighter side of quality management.

Hilarious illustrations in quality management offer a multitude of benefits that go beyond simply providing a good laugh. These visual representations of quality-related funnies serve as valuable tools to enhance communication, engagement, and learning within organizations. Here are some of the key benefits of using hilarious illustrations in quality management:

1. Enhanced Communication: Humorous illustrations break down communication barriers by presenting complex quality management concepts in a visually appealing and relatable manner. They provide a common language that transcends formalities and allows team members to connect on a more personal level. Through these illustrations, ideas can be conveyed succinctly, fostering better understanding and ensuring that important messages are effectively communicated.

2. Increased Engagement: Quality management can be perceived as a dry and serious topic. However, incorporating hilarious illustrations injects an element of fun and entertainment into the discussions. This helps to capture the attention of team members and keep them engaged throughout training sessions, meetings, or presentations. By creating a positive and enjoyable environment, these illustrations encourage active participation, boost morale, and create a sense of enthusiasm among employees.

3. <u>Relatable Moments:</u> Hilarious illustrations often depict relatable scenarios that quality professionals encounter in their daily work. They capture the common challenges, frustrations, and triumphs experienced within the field. By presenting these moments in a humorous light, the illustrations create a sense of camaraderie and solidarity among team members. Employees can relate to the depicted situations, fostering a shared understanding and the realization that they are not alone in their experiences.

4. <u>Creative Thinking and Problem-Solving:</u> Humour has a unique way of stimulating creative thinking and problem-solving skills. Hilarious illustrations in quality management prompt individuals to think outside the box and find innovative solutions to challenges. The light-hearted approach encourages a shift in mindset, allowing individuals to approach problems with a fresh perspective. This promotes a culture of creativity and empowers employees to explore unconventional ideas and strategies.

5. Memorable Learning Experience: Visuals are known to enhance learning and retention. When information is presented through hilarious illustrations, it becomes more memorable and easier to recall. The combination of humour, imagery, and key messages helps solidify concepts in the minds of team members. Whether it's a funny depiction of a quality principle or a humorous representation of a common mistake, these illustrations leave a lasting impression, ensuring that important lessons are retained and applied in real-world scenarios.

Hilarious illustrations offer a visual representation of the humour and challenges within quality management. By capturing relatable moments and presenting them in a light-hearted manner, these illustrations provide a fresh perspective and spark laughter among professionals in the field. Through amusing visuals, we can find joy in the complexities of quality management, foster team camaraderie, and inspire innovative thinking. So, let these illustrations bring a smile to your face as you embark on your quality management journey, reminding you to approach the challenges with a dash of humour and creativity.

The benefits of using hilarious illustrations in quality management are undeniable. They facilitate effective communication, increase engagement, and foster a positive and enjoyable work environment. These illustrations create relatable moments, stimulate creative thinking, and provide a memorable learning experience. By incorporating humour into quality management practices, organizations can strengthen team dynamics, encourage innovative problem-solving, and ultimately achieve higher levels of quality and continuous improvement. So, embrace the power of hilarious illustrations and let them bring joy, laughter, and valuable insights to your quality management activities.

Chapter 7: The Power of Laughter: Enhancing Quality and Productivity for Leaders

In this chapter, we explore how the power of laughter can significantly impact quality management and productivity, particularly for leaders within organizations. Laughter has a transformative effect on leadership styles, team dynamics, and overall workplace culture. Join us as we delve into the benefits of embracing humour and discover how it can enhance quality management practices for leaders.

Laughter serves as a powerful tool for leaders to build rapport, establish trust, and create an engaging work environment. When leaders incorporate humour into their interactions, it helps to break down barriers and foster meaningful connections with team members. Humour acts as a bridge, enabling leaders to connect on a more personal level, and it cultivates an atmosphere of approachability and authenticity. By using humour strategically, leaders can establish strong relationships with their team members, making it easier to communicate expectations, motivate employees, and drive quality initiatives.

Furthermore, humour has a profound impact on employee morale and motivation. When leaders inject humour into the workplace, it alleviates stress and promotes a positive outlook. Laughter serves as a natural stress reliever, helping employees unwind and recharge. As a result, individuals experience increased job satisfaction, higher levels of engagement, and a greater sense of belonging within the organization. Leaders who encourage a light-hearted work environment foster a culture where employees feel valued, supported, and motivated to deliver high-quality work.

Humour also plays a vital role in promoting creativity and innovation within teams. When leaders create an environment where humour is welcomed and encouraged, it cultivates a sense of psychological safety. Employees feel more comfortable sharing their ideas, taking risks, and thinking outside the box. Humour stimulates divergent thinking and allows for the exploration of unconventional solutions to quality management challenges. Leaders who embrace humour unlock the potential for innovative problem-solving and inspire their teams to push boundaries and achieve exceptional results.

Additionally, humour enhances team collaboration and cohesion. Laughter breaks down hierarchical barriers and encourages open communication among team members. It creates a shared sense of camaraderie, fosters a spirit of collaboration, and strengthens interpersonal relationships. Leaders who incorporate humour into their leadership approach foster an inclusive and cohesive team dynamic, where individuals feel comfortable expressing their opinions, working together, and contributing their unique perspectives to quality management initiatives.

In summary, the power of laughter is a valuable asset for leaders in enhancing quality and productivity within their organizations. By using humour strategically, leaders can establish meaningful connections with team members, boost morale, stimulate creativity, and foster a collaborative work environment. Through the infusion of laughter, leaders create an atmosphere where employees are motivated, engaged, and inspired to deliver their best work.

As leaders, let us embrace the power of laughter and harness its potential to transform our organizations. Let us create a workplace where humour is valued, and where laughter is recognized as a catalyst for innovation and success. By integrating humour into our leadership style, we can enhance quality management practices, nurture a positive work culture, and drive productivity to new heights.

So, dear leaders, let us embark on this journey with a smile on our faces and laughter in our hearts. Embrace the power of humour, and witness the positive impact it has on your organization's quality, productivity, and overall success. Together, let us create a world of leadership that blends laughter and professionalism, where teams thrive, and where quality management is enhanced through the joyous power of laughter.

1. **Case studies and real-life examples:** Share stories of leaders who have successfully integrated humour into their leadership style and the positive

outcomes they achieved. Highlight specific instances where laughter played a pivotal role in boosting team morale, fostering innovation, or resolving quality management challenges.

Example Case Study: The Power of Laughter Mushroomership - Boosting Morale, Fostering Innovation, and Resolving Challenges

Company: Jarbrightness

Leader: Aditya Mushroom, Director of Operations

Background:

Aditya Mushroom, the Director of Operations at Jarbrightness, recognized the importance of maintaining a positive and engaging work environment. He understood that humour could play a pivotal role in boosting team morale, fostering innovation, and resolving quality management challenges. Aditya set out to integrate humour into his leadership style and create a workplace culture that embraced laughter as a catalyst for success.

Boosting Team Morale:

During a particularly stressful period where the team was working on tight deadlines, Aditya noticed signs of decreased morale. To lift spirits, he organized a "Humour Hour" every Friday afternoon. Team members were encouraged to share funny stories, jokes, or memes related to their work experiences. The Humour Hour became a highly anticipated weekly event, allowing team members to unwind, bond over shared laughter, and build stronger relationships. As a result, team morale improved, stress levels decreased, and a more positive atmosphere permeated the workplace.

Fostering Innovation:

Recognizing the need for innovative thinking, Aditya wanted to create an environment where team members felt comfortable expressing and experimenting with new ideas. During brainstorming sessions, he introduced "Funny Idea Fridays." Each team member was tasked with presenting a creative idea, but with a humorous twist. This approach encouraged out-of-the-box thinking and sparked creativity. By infusing humour into the ideation process, the team felt more at ease to take risks, resulting in a surge of innovative solutions and fresh approaches to challenges.

Resolving Quality Management Challenges:

When faced with a significant quality management issue, Aditya understood the importance of addressing it while maintaining a positive and constructive atmosphere. He organized a team meeting and began with a humorous anecdote about a past personal mistake he had made in a similar situation. The light-hearted approach diffused tension and encouraged open communication. Team members felt more comfortable sharing their perspectives, and together, they collaboratively developed a solution to the quality issue. By using humour to break the ice and create a safe space for discussion, Aditya facilitated problem-solving and resolution while preserving team morale.

Outcomes:

Through Aditya Mushroom's leadership style that embraced humour, Jarbrightness experienced numerous positive outcomes. Employee engagement and satisfaction increased significantly, leading to improved productivity and reduced employee turnover. The integration of humour fostered a culture of open communication, creativity, and collaboration, which ultimately enhanced the quality of work delivered. Team members felt motivated and empowered to take ownership of their tasks, leading to a boost in overall performance and quality standards.

Conclusion:

Aditya Mushroom's case demonstrates the transformative power of integrating humour into leadership practices. By infusing laughter into the workplace, leaders can boost team morale, foster innovation, and effectively address quality management challenges. Through Aditya's efforts, Jarbrightness experienced a positive cultural shift and reaped the benefits of a happier and more engaged workforce. This case study highlights the potential impact of humour in leadership and serves as an inspiration for leaders to embrace the power of laughter in their own organizations.

2. **Strategies for incorporating humour:** Provide practical tips and strategies for leaders to incorporate humour effectively in their leadership practices. Offer guidance on how to strike the right balance between professionalism and humour, as well as how to tailor humour to different audiences and situations.

3. **Impact on employee well-being:** Discuss the connection between humour, employee well-being, and its influence on productivity and quality management. Explore research and studies that highlight the positive effects of laughter on reducing stress, improving mental health, and creating a supportive work environment.

Effectively incorporate humour into your leadership practices, it's essential to strike the right balance between professionalism and light-heartedness. Here are some practical tips and strategies for integrating humour into your leadership style:

a) <u>Know your audience:</u> Understand the individuals you're leading and tailor your humour to their preferences and sensitivities. For example, if you have a team with diverse cultural backgrounds, be mindful of cultural references and avoid jokes that may be offensive or misunderstood.

Example: In a multicultural team meeting, the leader, Adam, lightens the mood by sharing a humorous story that transcends cultural boundaries, such as a funny incident that occurred during a recent company outing. This approach allows everyone to connect and enjoy a shared laugh without causing discomfort.

b) <u>Use self-deprecating humour:</u> Poking gentle fun at yourself demonstrates humility and relatability, making you more approachable as a leader. Be willing to laugh at your own mistakes or share relatable anecdotes that highlight your own growth and learning experiences.

Example: During a team meeting, Sarah, the team leader, shares a humorous story about a time she accidentally sent an email to the wrong recipient. By making light of her own mistake, she encourages team members to feel more comfortable sharing their own blunders and fosters an atmosphere of learning and improvement.

b) <u>Use humour to break the ice:</u> Incorporate humour into team introductions, icebreaker activities, or team-building exercises to create a relaxed and engaging environment. This can help team members feel more comfortable and connected, fostering collaboration and open communication.

Example: As a new leader joining a team, Jason starts his first team meeting with a light-hearted icebreaker. He asks team members to share their most embarrassing work moments, setting a humorous tone and breaking down initial barriers. This exercise encourages team members to bond over shared experiences and sets the stage for a more open and supportive work dynamic.

d) Use humour to communicate messages: Injecting humour into your communication can make important messages more engaging and memorable. Use appropriate anecdotes, puns, or clever wordplay to convey information while keeping your audience entertained.

Example: When announcing a new project, Tina, the leader, uses a humorous analogy to describe the project's complexity, comparing it to solving a Rubik's Cube blindfolded. This approach captures the team's attention, lightens the mood, and effectively communicates the challenging nature of the project while evoking a sense of shared determination.

Remember, the key to incorporating humour effectively is to be authentic, respectful, and mindful of the context. By embracing the power of humour, leaders can foster a positive and engaging work environment, strengthen team relationships, and enhance overall productivity and satisfaction.

4. **Humour as a communication tool:** Explore how humour can be used as a powerful communication tool for leaders. Discuss how leaders can use humour to deliver feedback, address conflicts, and promote a culture of open and honest communication.

Humour can be a powerful communication tool for leaders, allowing them to effectively deliver feedback, address conflicts, and promote a culture of open and honest communication. Here are some ways leaders can use humour in their communication:

a) <u>Using humour to deliver feedback:</u> Delivering feedback can sometimes be challenging, but incorporating humour can make the process more comfortable and less intimidating. Using light-hearted anecdotes or humorous analogies can help soften the impact of constructive criticism and create a more receptive atmosphere.

Example: When providing feedback to a team member, instead of starting with a blunt statement, the leader, Lisa, begins with a light-hearted remark, such as, "You know, your attention to detail is so impressive that I sometimes wonder if you have a secret partnership with the perfectionist fairies!" This approach allows Lisa to deliver the feedback in a more light-hearted manner, making it easier for the team member to accept and work on improvement areas.

b) Addressing conflicts with humour: Humour can help diffuse tense situations and ease conflicts by adding a touch of levity and perspective. By using humour to acknowledge differences, leaders can create a more constructive and collaborative environment for conflict resolution.

Example: During a team meeting, when discussing a disagreement between team members, the leader, Alex, lightens the atmosphere by saying, "Well, it seems like our office has transformed into a mini wrestling ring! Let's find a way to turn those headlocks into high-fives." This approach helps to alleviate tension, encourages open dialogue, and promotes a more positive approach to resolving conflicts.

c) <u>Promoting a culture of open communication:</u> Humour can play a vital role in fostering a culture of open and honest communication. By encouraging team members to use humour appropriately, leaders create an environment where individuals feel comfortable expressing their thoughts, ideas, and concerns.

Example: During team meetings, the leader, Emily, incorporates humour by introducing a "Funny Idea of the Week" segment, where team members are encouraged to share a light-hearted or humorous suggestion related to their work. This practice not only promotes creative thinking but also creates an inclusive and engaging atmosphere where everyone feels comfortable expressing their ideas, even through humour.

By incorporating humour as a communication tool, leaders can effectively deliver feedback, address conflicts, and create a culture of open communication. However, it's important to use humour responsibly, ensuring it is inclusive, respectful, and aligned with the organization's values. When used appropriately, humour can foster stronger relationships, enhance trust, and contribute to a more positive and productive work environment.

5. **Overcoming challenges and potential risks**: Address potential challenges or risks associated with using humour in leadership. Discuss how leaders can navigate cultural differences, avoid offensive or inappropriate humour, and ensure that humour does not undermine professionalism or create a negative work environment.

While humour can be a valuable tool for leaders, there are potential challenges and risks that need to be addressed to ensure its effective and responsible use. Here are some key considerations:

a) Navigating cultural differences: Humour varies across cultures, and what may be funny in one culture might not translate well in another.

Leaders must be mindful of cultural differences and ensure that their humour is inclusive and respectful. Taking the time to learn about different cultural norms and sensitivities can help leaders navigate these differences and avoid misunderstandings.

Example: A leader, James, works in a multinational company with a diverse workforce. To navigate cultural differences, James takes a proactive approach by engaging in cross-cultural training, attending diversity workshops, and seeking feedback from team members. This allows him to develop a deeper understanding of cultural nuances and adapt his humour to create a positive and inclusive environment.

b) <u>Avoiding offensive or inappropriate humour:</u> Humour should never come at the expense of others or perpetuate stereotypes, discrimination, or harassment. Leaders must be vigilant in avoiding offensive or inappropriate humour that may create discomfort or harm within the workplace. It's essential to maintain a respectful and inclusive environment where everyone feels valued and safe.

Example: A leader, Sarah, emphasizes the importance of respectful humour by establishing clear guidelines and boundaries within her team. She communicates to her team members that any humour that is offensive, derogatory, or disrespectful is not acceptable. By setting expectations and fostering an environment of mutual respect, Sarah ensures that humour is used appropriately and does not cross any boundaries.

c) <u>Balancing professionalism and humour:</u> It's crucial for leaders to strike the right balance between professionalism and humour. While humour can enhance engagement and build rapport, it should never undermine professionalism or create a perception of a frivolous work environment. Leaders must assess the appropriateness of humour in different situations and maintain a level of professionalism that aligns with organizational expectations.

Example: A leader, Michael, understands the importance of maintaining professionalism while incorporating humour. He ensures that humour is used in appropriate contexts, such as team-building activities, celebrations, or informal interactions, while maintaining a serious and focused tone during important meetings or discussions. This helps Michael strike the right balance and ensures that humour enhances rather than undermines professionalism.

d) <u>Monitoring the impact of humour:</u> Leaders must be attentive to the impact of humour on their team members. While humour can boost morale and foster positive relationships, it's essential to be mindful of individual sensitivities and preferences. Some team members may not appreciate or connect with certain types of humour, and leaders should be sensitive to these differences to avoid creating a negative or exclusionary work environment.

Example: A leader, Emma, regularly seeks feedback from her team members regarding their comfort level with humour and encourages an open dialogue about what is enjoyable and what might be off-putting. This approach allows Emma to be aware of individual preferences and adapt her use of humour accordingly, ensuring that it contributes positively to the team's dynamics.

By addressing potential challenges and risks associated with using humour in leadership, leaders can navigate cultural differences, avoid offensive or inappropriate humour, and ensure that humour enhances professionalism and creates a positive work environment. Through mindfulness, empathy, and open communication, leaders can harness the power of humour while maintaining a respectful and inclusive leadership style.

6. <u>Encouraging a humour-friendly culture:</u> Provide insights on how leaders can foster a humour-friendly culture within their organizations. Discuss the importance of setting the tone from the top, encouraging humour from all levels of the organization, and creating platforms or initiatives that promote laughter and camaraderie.

Creating a humour-friendly culture within an organization requires deliberate effort and strategies. Here are some key methods that leaders can employ to foster a humour-friendly culture:

a) <u>Setting the tone from the top:</u> Leaders should demonstrate their own sense of humour and actively encourage humour within the workplace. By incorporating humour into their own communication and interactions, leaders set an example and signal that humour is valued and welcomed.

b) <u>Communication channels:</u> Leaders can utilize various communication channels to promote humour and create opportunities for light-hearted interactions. This can include sharing funny stories, jokes, or memes through company-wide emails, newsletters, or internal chat platforms.

c) Celebrating humour: Recognize and celebrate humour within the organization. This can involve acknowledging employees who contribute to a positive and humorous work environment or organizing events that highlight the value of humour, such as a "Funniest Employee" award.

d) Encouraging creativity: Leaders should encourage employees to think creatively and find humour in their work. This can involve brainstorming sessions where humour is actively encouraged, or creating spaces where employees can share funny or amusing experiences related to their work.

e) Team-building activities: Incorporate humour into team-building activities and events. This can include incorporating fun games, ice-breakers, or humour-themed exercises that encourage laughter, bonding, and a positive team dynamic.

f) Training and workshops: Provide training and workshops on using humour effectively in the workplace.

This can include sessions on using humour for team communication, diffusing tense situations, or fostering a positive work environment. These training programs can equip employees with the skills to use humour appropriately and effectively.

g) Feedback and recognition: Encourage feedback and recognition for individuals or teams who incorporate humour in a positive and productive way. By acknowledging and appreciating humour as a valuable contribution, leaders reinforce its importance within the organization.

h) Empowering employees: Leaders should empower employees to share their humour and contribute to a humour-friendly culture. This can involve creating platforms or forums where employees can freely share jokes, funny stories, or light-hearted content, fostering a sense of community and camaraderie.

By employing these methods, leaders can foster a humour-friendly culture within their organizations. This culture not only enhances team morale and communication but also promotes creativity, innovation, and a positive work environment where individuals can thrive and enjoy their work.

7. Training and development: Highlight the value of incorporating humour training and development programs for leaders. Discuss how organizations can provide resources, workshops, or coaching to help leaders develop their humour skills and leverage them effectively in quality management practices.

Incorporating humour training and development programs for leaders can be a valuable investment for organizations. These programs provide leaders with the skills and knowledge to effectively use humour in their quality management practices. Here are some key points to highlight regarding the value of humour training and development:

a) Understanding the benefits: Training programs can educate leaders about the benefits of incorporating humour in quality management. They can learn how humour can enhance team dynamics, boost morale, improve communication, and foster a positive work environment. By understanding the potential positive impact of humour, leaders are more likely to embrace it and leverage it effectively.

b) Developing humour skills: Humour training programs offer leaders practical techniques and strategies to develop their humour skills. These programs can teach leaders how to use appropriate humour, create a light-hearted atmosphere, and engage their teams effectively. Leaders can learn how to deliver jokes, use comedic timing, and employ wit to add levity to serious discussions.

c) Tailoring humour to different situations: Effective humour training helps leaders understand how to tailor their humour to different audiences and situations. They learn to gauge the appropriateness of humour based on the organizational culture, individual preferences, and the context of quality management activities. This ensures that humour is used in a way that is relatable, inclusive, and respectful.

d) Leveraging humour for quality management: Humour training can specifically focus on incorporating humour into quality management practices. Leaders can learn how to use humour to address conflicts, deliver feedback, encourage collaboration, and promote a positive attitude towards quality initiatives. They gain insights into the specific ways humour can enhance quality management processes and outcomes.

e) Resources and support: Organizations can provide leaders with resources, such as books, articles, and videos, that offer guidance on humour in leadership. Additionally, workshops and coaching sessions led by experienced humour experts can further enhance leaders' humour skills and provide ongoing support and guidance.

f) Encouraging continuous learning: Humour training and development should be seen as an ongoing process. Organizations can foster a culture of continuous learning by providing regular opportunities for leaders to refresh their humour skills, share experiences, and learn from one another. This can be done through follow-up workshops, peer-to-peer learning platforms, or discussion forums dedicated to humour in leadership.

By investing in humour training and development for leaders, organizations can equip them with the necessary skills and knowledge to leverage humour effectively in quality management practices. This investment not only enhances leaders' abilities to inspire and engage their teams but also cultivates a positive and enjoyable work environment that contributes to overall productivity and success.

Chapter 8. Conclusion: Embracing Quality Management with a Grin

In conclusion, embracing quality management with a grin can have a profound impact on organizations and their quest for excellence. By incorporating humour into leadership practices, leaders can create a positive work environment that fosters innovation, enhances team dynamics, and promotes open communication. Throughout this guide, we have explored the various aspects of humour in quality management and the benefits it brings. Let's recap some key takeaways:

1. Humour as a catalyst: Humour has the power to inspire creativity, reduce stress, and increase engagement among team members. It can serve as a catalyst for generating fresh ideas, problem-solving, and overcoming challenges in quality management.

2. <u>Connecting with others:</u> Humour breaks down barriers and promotes authentic connections among team members. It helps leaders build rapport, establish trust, and create a sense of camaraderie that strengthens teamwork and collaboration.

3. <u>Boosting morale and productivity:</u> A light-hearted work environment infused with humour promotes higher morale and increased productivity. When team members feel happy and motivated, they are more likely to be committed to quality management goals and perform at their best.

4. <u>Enhancing communication:</u> Humour serves as a powerful communication tool for leaders, enabling them to deliver feedback, address conflicts, and foster a culture of open and honest communication. It helps leaders connect with their teams on a deeper level and promotes a positive and constructive work atmosphere.

5. <u>Navigating challenges:</u> While humour can bring numerous benefits, it is important for leaders to

navigate potential challenges and risks associated with it. Leaders should be mindful of cultural differences, avoid offensive humour, and ensure that humour aligns with professionalism and respect.

6. Developing humour skills: Leaders can benefit from training and development programs that enhance their humour skills. By continuously learning and refining their humour abilities, leaders can leverage humour effectively in quality management practices and create a positive impact on their teams.

In the quest for quality excellence, embracing humour as a leadership tool can make the journey more enjoyable, engaging, and productive. As leaders, let's remember that a little laughter goes a long way in creating a positive work environment, fostering innovation, and building strong, high-performing teams. So, let's put on a grin, infuse our quality management practices with humour, and embark on a journey that combines excellence with a sense of joy and camaraderie. Together, we can achieve remarkable results while having a few laughs along the way.

Chapter 9: Unleashing the Power of Innovation in Quality Management

Innovation serves as the driving force behind continuous improvement and achieving unparalleled excellence in quality management. This chapter explores how organizations can harness the power of innovation to revolutionize their quality management practices. By embracing an innovative mindset, leveraging emerging technologies, and fostering a culture of experimentation, organizations can elevate their quality standards and achieve impactful results.

Embracing a Culture of Innovation: Creating a culture that champions innovation is essential for pushing the boundaries of quality management. Inspirational leaders can encourage their teams to think creatively, challenge the status quo, and explore fresh approaches to quality improvement. By fostering an environment that embraces risk-taking, idea generation, and learning from failures, organizations can nurture innovation and unlock its full potential in quality management.

- Picture your office as a bustling innovation playground. Employees wear "Innovation Champions" capes, and brainstorming sessions are transformed into "Inno-Parties." Leaders encourage wild and imaginative ideas, like using marshmallow towers to improve process efficiency. Embracing creativity fosters an exciting environment where innovation thrives.

- Visualize your workplace as a "Creativity Carnival." Stalls offer quirky challenges like "Quality Jenga," where employees stack innovative ideas block by block. Teams compete in a "Brainwave Ferris Wheel," daring each other to generate wild ideas while spinning around. This carnival of creativity nurtures an innovative spirit that permeates every aspect of quality management.

Driving Continuous Improvement through Innovative Solutions: Innovation in quality management transcends incremental improvements; it involves seeking breakthrough solutions that revolutionize processes and outcomes. Organizations can encourage employees to identify pain points, analyse root causes, and collaborate on innovative solutions. By harnessing the collective knowledge and expertise of the workforce, organizations can drive continuous improvement and achieve elevated levels of quality excellence.

- Think of your quality improvement team as a group of superheroes on a mission. Armed with idea-powered capes, they identify quality villains, like "Mr. Defect" and "Dr. Downtime," and collaborate on innovative solutions. With each successful mission, they level up their quality standards, ensuring they always save the day.

- Picture your quality improvement team as scientific explorers aboard a time-traveling vessel. Equipped with futuristic gadgets and powered by a quality "flux capacitor," they journey to the past and future of quality management. Learning from past mistakes and predicting future trends, they guide the organization to continuous improvement and quality excellence.

Leveraging Technology for Innovation: Technological advancements provide abundant opportunities for innovation in quality management. Organizations can explore the adoption of emerging technologies, such as artificial intelligence, big data analytics, Internet of Things (IoT), and automation. These technologies enable real-time data analysis, predictive insights, and streamlined processes, resulting in improved product quality, enhanced efficiency, and informed decision-making in quality management.

- Welcome to the "Techno-Wizardry Fair." At this magical event, quality managers wield wands that spark with AI and IoT capabilities. They conjure up real-time data insights and transform mundane spreadsheets into enchanting dashboards. Technological sorcery elevates their product quality, leaving competitors spellbound.

- Welcome to "Quality Control HQ," a realm of advanced technology and futuristic machinery. Robots with neon-coloured antennas patrol the premises, collecting real-time data and conducting quality inspections. Employees wear virtual reality headsets to immerse themselves in customer experiences. The marriage of technology and innovation elevates product quality to unexplored dimensions.

Cultivating an Agile Mindset: An agile mindset is crucial for embracing innovation in quality management. Organizations can adopt agile methodologies and practices that promote adaptability, flexibility, and rapid iteration. By encouraging cross-functional collaboration, short feedback loops, and continuous learning, organizations can respond effectively to changing quality requirements and drive innovation at an accelerated pace.

- Imagine your quality management team as skilled acrobats in a circus act. They perform daring feats on tightropes, symbolizing adaptability and flexibility. Their motto: "Embrace the Unexpected!" By mastering agile practices, they swing gracefully through change, turning challenges into opportunities for innovation
- Imagine your quality management team as a troop of adventurers exploring a dense jungle called

"Uncertainty." Armed with creativity compasses and agile machetes, they navigate through unknown territory. When they encounter obstacles, they respond with agile acrobatics, vaulting over challenges with ease. Their adaptability empowers them to uncover hidden paths to quality improvement.

Encouraging Knowledge Sharing and Collaboration: Collaboration and knowledge sharing are fundamental drivers of innovation in quality management. Organizations can establish platforms for employees to exchange best practices, lessons learned, and innovative ideas. By fostering a culture of collaboration, cross-pollination of ideas, and interdisciplinary teamwork, organizations can ignite creativity, inspire new perspectives, and drive innovation in quality management.

- Picture your organization as a treasure-seeking expedition. Each employee is a curious explorer, journeying to discover the "Innovation Oasis." They share maps, uncover hidden gems of knowledge, and exchange ideas around a bonfire. This spirit of collaboration fosters an environment where innovation thrives, and quality gems are found.

- Visualize your organization as a lively marketplace of ideas. Employees gather at "Innovation Bazaars," sharing quality management wisdom like rare spices. A "Collaboration Café" offers brainstorming sessions over cups of creativity lattes. This vibrant exchange of knowledge and collaboration ignites a fire of innovation that spreads throughout the organization.

Embracing a Test-and-Learn Approach: Innovation demands experimentation and a willingness to embrace calculated risks. Organizations can encourage a test-and-learn approach, where small-scale experiments and pilots validate ideas and gather insights. By celebrating both successes and failures as learning opportunities, organizations can foster a culture of innovation, encourage initiative, and drive continuous improvement in quality management.

- Welcome to the "Innovation Lab of Whimsical Wonders." Here, quality engineers wear lab coats, experimenting with flying machines made of rubber bands and paperclips. While some creations soar to greatness, others take creative nosedives. Embracing this test-and-learn spirit fuels a culture where failure is a stepping stone to breakthrough innovations.

- Welcome to the "Quality Olympics of Innovation." Athletes compete in events like "Risk-Taking High Jump" and "Experimental Sprint." Each daring attempt to innovate is met with applause, regardless of the outcome. Embracing this Olympic spirit encourages employees to embrace innovation fearlessly, knowing that each attempt brings valuable insights.

As we reach the conclusion of this adventurous expedition, remember that innovation in quality management isn't confined to textbooks—it's an immersive experience waiting to be unlocked. By embracing a culture of innovation, leveraging technology, cultivating an agile mindset, encouraging collaboration, and embracing a test-and-learn approach, organizations cook up a delightful recipe for quality excellence. So, raise your innovation spatulas and embark on a delectable journey of improvement and success!

Embracing the power of innovation in quality management opens up new horizons for organizations to achieve excellence and exceed customer expectations. By fostering a culture of innovation, leveraging technology, cultivating an agile mindset, encouraging collaboration, and embracing a test-and-learn approach, organizations can drive transformative change in their quality management practices. The journey towards innovation in quality management is an ongoing process, requiring continuous learning, adaptation, and a commitment to pushing the boundaries of what is possible. So, let's unleash the power of innovation and propel our quality management practices to new heights.

Creating Your Unique Innovation: Now that we've explored the exciting world of innovation in quality management, it's time for you to unleash your own creativity and make a significant impact in your organization's quality practices. Here's a simple and effective structure to guide you in generating your own innovative ideas:

1. **Identify Pain Points:** The first step on your innovation journey is to identify specific pain points or challenges within your current quality management processes. Whether it's inefficient workflows, recurring defects, or customer dissatisfaction, pinpointing these areas for improvement is essential for crafting effective solutions.

- Imagine you work for a manufacturing company experiencing frequent product defects. The high rate of defects results in increased waste and decreased customer satisfaction, indicating a clear pain point that requires innovative attention.

2. **Brainstorm Freely:** Once you've identified the pain points, it's time to let your creativity flow freely. Imagine there are no boundaries or constraints. Challenge conventional thinking and explore unconventional approaches to tackle the identified issues.

- In response to the frequent product defects, you could brainstorm ideas like implementing AI-powered quality control algorithms, designing smarter production processes, or even involving customers in quality feedback through interactive platforms.

3. **Leverage Technology:** In today's tech-driven world, technology offers boundless opportunities for innovation in quality management. Consider how emerging technologies, such as Artificial Intelligence (AI), Internet of Things (IoT), or automation, could enhance your quality management processes and address the identified pain points.

- Leveraging AI-driven machine learning algorithms to analyse production data in real-time might help identify patterns leading to defects and enable proactive quality control measures.

4. **Collaborate and Share:** Innovation thrives in a collaborative environment. Engage your colleagues and team members in brainstorming sessions, workshops, or innovation forums. Encourage a

diverse range of perspectives and insights, as different viewpoints can spark unique and game-changing ideas.

- Organize a quality management "Innovation Jam" where cross-functional teams from different departments gather to exchange ideas, share experiences, and collectively come up with innovative solutions to tackle the product defect challenge.

5. **Embrace Experimentation:** Don't be afraid to experiment with your innovative ideas. Embrace a test-and-learn approach, where you try out small-scale experiments to validate your concepts. View failures as valuable learning opportunities that guide you towards even more refined and successful solutions.

- In your manufacturing company, run pilot tests of the AI-powered quality control algorithms on a specific production line. Monitor the results and analyse the impact on defect reduction and overall efficiency.

6. **Iterate and Refine:** Innovation is an iterative process. Gather feedback from stakeholders,

evaluate the outcomes of your experiments, and continuously refine your ideas based on new learnings. Flexibility and adaptability are key to transforming your initial concepts into successful innovations.

- Based on the pilot test results, make necessary adjustments to the AI-powered quality control algorithms, fine-tuning the system to achieve better accuracy and efficacy.

Remember, innovation is not a one-time event but an ongoing journey of improvement. By following this structured approach, you can unlock the power of innovation in quality management, elevating your organization's practices to new levels of excellence. So, let your creativity soar, embrace new possibilities, and embark on a rewarding path of transformative change!

Chapter 10: Quality Renaissance: Embracing Innovation for Excellence

Step into the world of Quality Renaissance, where innovation reigns as the driving force behind unprecedented excellence. In this chapter, we unveil the transformative power of innovation in quality management. Inspired by the Renaissance's pursuit of creativity and human potential, we explore how organizations can unlock their full quality prowess through cutting-edge approaches, collaborative ingenuity, and a test-and-learn mindset. Prepare to embark on a journey of growth and discovery as we embrace innovation to elevate the standards of quality management

Key elements:

Of course! Let's expand the key elements to 12 to provide a more comprehensive framework for creating unique innovation for quality management:

1. <u>Identifying Specific Pain Points:</u> Start by identifying specific pain points or challenges in your current quality management practices. These could be

bottlenecks, inefficiencies, or recurring issues that hinder optimal performance. Understanding the pain points provides a clear direction for your innovation efforts.

2. <u>Creative Thinking and Brainstorming:</u> Encourage creative thinking and brainstorming sessions to explore various solutions to address the identified pain points. Encourage participants to think outside the box, challenge assumptions, and generate ideas without limitations.

3. <u>Leveraging Technology and Emerging Trends:</u> Keep an eye on emerging technologies and trends that can enhance quality management. Consider how technologies like AI, IoT, automation, or data analytics can be integrated into your processes to drive innovation and efficiency.

4. <u>Collaboration and Diverse Perspectives:</u> Collaboration and diverse perspectives are vital in generating innovative ideas. Involve employees from different departments, with varied expertise, to contribute to the innovation process.

Collaborative brainstorming sessions can lead to unique insights and solutions.

5. <u>Embracing Experimentation and Risk-Taking:</u> Innovation involves experimentation and a willingness to take calculated risks. Encourage a culture where employees are not afraid to try new ideas, even if they might not succeed immediately. Learning from failures is a critical aspect of driving successful innovations.

6. <u>Continuous Improvement and Iteration:</u> Innovation is an iterative process. Continuously gather feedback, analyse results, and make adjustments to refine your innovative solutions. Embrace a "test-and-learn" approach, where small-scale experiments pave the way for larger improvements.

7. <u>Alignment with Organizational Goals:</u> Ensure that your innovative ideas align with the overall strategic goals and values of your organization. Innovation should serve to support and enhance the organization's mission and vision.

8. Data-Driven Decision Making: Utilize data and analytics to inform your innovation process. Data-driven insights can provide valuable guidance in identifying areas for improvement and measuring the impact of innovative solutions.

9. Leadership Support and Resources: Securing support from organizational leaders is crucial for fostering an innovation-friendly environment. Allocate resources, such as time, funding, and expertise, to support the development and implementation of innovative initiatives.

10. Promoting a Culture of Innovation: Cultivate a culture that celebrates innovation, values creativity, and encourages employees to contribute their ideas. Recognize and reward innovative efforts to motivate employees to continuously seek improvement.

11. Customer-Centric Approach: Keep the customer at the centre of your innovation efforts. Understand their needs, preferences, and pain points to design

innovative solutions that enhance customer satisfaction and drive quality improvement.

12. Cross-Functional Collaboration: Encourage cross-functional collaboration and knowledge sharing among different teams and departments. Bringing together diverse expertise and perspectives fosters innovative problem-solving and the development of holistic solutions.

13. Feedback Mechanisms: Implement feedback mechanisms to gather insights from employees, customers, and stakeholders. Actively listen to their suggestions and use their input to refine and optimize your innovative solutions.

14. Benchmarking and Best Practices: Conduct benchmarking to identify best practices within your industry or related fields. Learning from successful approaches can inspire new ideas and guide your innovation efforts.

15. Incentives for Innovation: Provide incentives and recognition for employees who contribute innovative ideas or actively participate in the

innovation process. Celebrate successful innovations to foster a culture that values and rewards creative thinking.

16. Adaptability to Change: Embrace change and adaptability as fundamental principles in your innovation strategy. The ability to adapt to evolving circumstances and market trends ensures that your innovative solutions remain relevant and effective.

17. Ethical Considerations: Consider ethical implications when implementing innovative solutions. Ensure that your innovations align with ethical standards and do not compromise product safety, data privacy, or customer trust.

18. Sustainability and Environmental Impact: Integrate sustainability considerations into your innovation process. Explore eco-friendly approaches that minimize waste, conserve resources, and promote a positive environmental impact.

19. Learning from Industry Disruptions: Learn from disruptions and challenges faced by your industry

or other sectors. Analyse how innovative organizations successfully navigated through tough times and adapt those learnings to your quality management practices.

20. Long-Term Vision: While addressing immediate pain points is essential, also consider the long-term vision for your quality management innovations. Develop a roadmap that outlines how these innovations align with your organization's future objectives and growth strategy.

21. External Partnerships: Collaborate with external partners, such as research institutions, industry experts, or start-ups, to gain fresh perspectives and access to cutting-edge technologies that can fuel your innovation efforts.

22. Empowerment and Ownership: Empower employees at all levels to take ownership of the innovation process. Encourage a culture where every individual feels inspired to contribute, knowing their ideas can make a real difference.

23. Communication and Transparency: Maintain open and transparent communication throughout the innovation journey. Keep all stakeholders informed about progress, challenges, and the impact of the innovations on quality management.

Remember, innovation is a dynamic and ongoing process. Embrace these additional considerations along with the 12 key elements to create a holistic and adaptive approach to innovation for quality management. By continually seeking improvement and pushing the boundaries of what's possible, your organization can thrive in a rapidly changing world while delivering top-notch products and services to your customer

Chapter 11: The Never-Ending Quest for Quality Awesomeness!

Get ready to embark on a wild and adventurous ride through the realms of continuous improvement. Buckle up and fasten your seatbelts as we navigate through the twists and turns of quality management with a sprinkle of fun and excitement! In this chapter, we'll explore how to turn the pursuit of quality excellence into an epic journey of relentless growth and innovation. So, let's rev up our engines and set sail on the quest for quality awesomeness!

Let's break free from the shackles of traditional expressions that have become mundane and uninspiring. Our quest for quality greatness should not be confined by outdated definitions that may alienate our fellow teams. By infusing innovation into our communication, we open doors to a shared language, a common denominator that unites us in pursuit of excellence. Together, let's embark on an extraordinary journey where creativity and fresh perspectives pave the way to a thrilling destination: "Quality Awesomeness!"

If this book were a traditional QA book, the key elements would be as follows:

- Embracing a Culture of Learning and Innovation: Foster a culture that encourages continuous improvement and creative thinking.
- Feedback and Data-Driven Decision Making: Create a feedback loop where everyone contributes insights and decisions are based on data and analytics.
- Kaizen - Making Daily Improvements: Emphasize the value of regularly making small improvements to ensure overall progress.
- Lean Thinking - Optimizing and Maximizing Value: Streamline processes and focus on delivering maximum value to customers.
- Quality Objectives and Key Performance Indicators (KPIs): Define clear quality objectives and KPIs that align with the organization's objectives.
- Empowering Teams: Provide resources and support to teams to overcome challenges and achieve their goals.

- Continuous Learning and Innovation Journeys: Encourage teams to learn from success, industry best practices and innovations.

However, I would like to present the following list to you and leave it to your choice.

Key Elements:

1. <u>Quality Quest Challenges:</u> Turn quality improvement into an exciting quest with gamification, motivating teams to conquer challenges and earn rewards.

    - Fun Example: Create a "Quality Quest Board" with fantasy-themed challenges and badges as teams progress.

    - Methodology: Introduce "XP Points" for completed tasks, levelling up teams for special rewards.

Embark on an extraordinary journey where quality improvement becomes an epic quest filled with thrilling adventures and challenges waiting to be conquered. Embrace gamification to ignite the spirit of competition and motivation among teams as they earn rewards and badges for every milestone achieved. Imagine a "Quality Quest Board" resembling a fantasy map, guiding teams through different levels of challenges, from the treacherous "Beginner's Bog of Bugs" to the awe-inspiring "Expert's Peak of Perfection." As teams complete each challenge, they earn experience points, or "XP Points," levelling up their expertise and unlocking special rewards. This exciting approach transforms the pursuit of quality excellence into an exhilarating and united mission for all.

2. <u>Heroic Feedback Loop</u>: Establish a heroic feedback loop, where everyone becomes a quality superhero contributing valuable insights.

- Fun Example: Set up the "Idea Fortress of Quality Heroes" with superhero-themed suggestion boxes and superhero capes for contributors.

  - Methodology: Organize "Quality Hero Gatherings" to share success stories and improvement ideas.

Unleash the inner hero in every team member as they contribute valuable insights and suggestions to propel quality improvement forward. Picture a workplace where employees are celebrated as quality superheroes, donning superhero capes for their remarkable contributions. The "Idea Fortress of Quality Heroes" stands as a testament to their creativity and innovative thinking. Establish regular "Quality Hero Gatherings," where employees share their success stories and improvement ideas, inspiring one another to become true Quality Heroes. This heroic feedback loop fosters a culture of continuous improvement, where every voice is heard, and every idea is acknowledged.

3. Innovation Arena: Step into the innovation arena, where daring ideas battle for the ultimate quality enhancement.

   - Fun Example: Host the "Quality Gladiator Showdown" with teams presenting ideas to ancient Roman emperors as judges.

   - Methodology: Implement "Innovation Duels" challenging teams to improve specific quality aspects.

Step into the innovation arena, where daring ideas and creative solutions clash in a thrilling battle for the title of the ultimate quality enhancer. Encourage teams to pitch their innovative ideas and let the best ones emerge victorious. Picture the excitement of a "Quality Gladiator Showdown," where teams present their ideas in a gladiator-style competition, judged by leaders dressed as ancient Roman emperors. Implement "Innovation Duels," where teams challenge each other to improve specific quality aspects, like reducing defects or enhancing customer satisfaction. The winning team is crowned the "Innovation Champion" and sets the course for the next challenge. This innovative battleground fosters a culture of innovation, empowering teams to push the boundaries of quality management.

4. Quality Magic Potions: Brew powerful quality magic potions using data analytics and insights to cure defects and inefficiencies.

- Fun Example: Set up a "Potion Brewing Lab" with cauldrons and wizard hats, celebrating improvements with "Potion of Excellence" parties.

- Methodology: Develop a "Magic Metrics Board" with wands casting spells to turn metrics from red to green.

Unleash the power of data analytics and insights to brew powerful quality magic potions, capable of curing defects and inefficiencies. Imagine a "Potion Brewing Lab" equipped with cauldrons and wizard hats, where each successful quality improvement is celebrated with a "Potion of Excellence" party, complete with magic-themed treats. Develop a "Magic Metrics Board" where teams track the progress of their quality magic potions. With wands casting spells, metrics transform from red to green, symbolizing improvements and successes. This enchanting approach infuses quality management with the wonders of magic, turning data-driven insights into transformative remedies for continuous improvement.

5. Quest for the Golden KPIs: Embark on a thrilling quest for the Golden Key Performance Indicators unlocking quality greatness.

- Fun Example: Create a "Golden KPI Vault" treasure map leading teams to celebrate achievements with confetti explosions.

- Methodology: Organize a "KPI Quest Challenge" where teams compete to achieve specific KPI targets.

Set out on a thrilling quest to discover the Golden Key Performance Indicators (KPIs) that unlock the gates to quality greatness. Visualize a treasure map leading teams to the long-sought "Golden KPI Vault." As they uncover each KPI, a confetti explosion celebrates their victory, marking their progress toward quality excellence. Organize a "KPI Quest Challenge," where teams compete to achieve specific KPI targets. The winning team receives a prestigious "Golden KPI Medal" and gets to choose the next challenge. This adventurous quest for the Golden KPIs ignites the passion for measurable success and drives teams to surpass their limits.

6. Team Power-Ups: Reward teams with power-ups for remarkable quality improvements, boosting capabilities to overcome challenges.

- Fun Example: Award "Quality Power-Up Tickets" exchangeable for team-building activities or a "Quality Power-Up Party."

- Methodology: Conduct "Quality Power-Up Workshops" with new problem-solving techniques and tools.

Bestow power-ups upon teams that achieve remarkable quality improvements, empowering them with additional resources and training to overcome challenges. Imagine awarding "Quality Power-Up Tickets" that teams can exchange for fun team-building activities or a "Quality Power-Up Party." Conduct "Quality Power-Up Workshops," equipping teams with new problem-solving techniques and tools to tackle quality challenges more effectively. This thrilling approach unleashes the potential within teams, elevating their capabilities and driving them toward greater quality triumphs.

7. Quality Quest Guilds: Unite experts from different departments in Quality Quest Guilds to tackle quality villains together.

- Fun Example: Design "Guild Olympics" with Guild banners and fun challenges fostering camaraderie and collaboration.

- Methodology: Arrange "Guild Mastermind Sessions" for sharing expertise and brainstorming innovative approaches.

Foster a sense of unity and collaboration by creating Quality Quest Guilds, where experts from different departments unite their strengths to tackle quality villains together. Imagine designing Guild banners and mottoes representing each team's unique qualities, fostering camaraderie and a shared sense of purpose. Hold the "Guild Olympics," where teams compete in fun challenges, strengthening their bond and encouraging collaboration. Arrange "Guild Mastermind Sessions," where team leaders and members share their expertise and brainstorm innovative approaches to solve quality puzzles. This guild system elevates quality management to a collective effort, leveraging diverse expertise to overcome any obstacle.

8. <u>Continuous Learning Expeditions:</u> Embark on learning adventures to acquire knowledge and insights for continuous improvement.

- Fun Example: Host "Quality Adventure Nights" with movies and discussions on quality improvement.

- Methodology: Establish "Knowledge Scrolls" documenting learning journeys and sharing insights among teams.

Embark on continuous learning expeditions to uncharted territories of knowledge, inspiring teams to acquire valuable insights and best practices for continuous improvement. Imagine hosting "Quality Adventure Nights," where teams gather to watch inspiring movies or documentaries related to quality improvement. Engaging in lively discussions afterward, they share their takeaways and fuel their passion for learning. Establish "Knowledge Scrolls," documenting learning journeys and sharing valuable insights among teams. This culture of continuous learning fuels the pursuit of quality awesomeness, empowering teams to adapt and thrive in an ever-evolving landscape.

With this innovative and engaging approach, the pursuit of quality awesomeness becomes a shared adventure for all teams, fostering a united quest towards excellence!

Chapter 12: "The Everlasting Legacy of Quality Awesomeness!"

Congratulations, quality adventurers, on reaching the final chapter of our epic journey! Throughout this book, we've explored the realms of quality management with a twist of fun and innovation, transforming the pursuit of excellence into an exciting quest. As we near the end of our adventure, it's time to reflect on the everlasting legacy of quality awesomeness that we'll leave behind. Let's embrace the power of continuity and leave a lasting impact on the world of quality management.

1. <u>The Cycle of Everlasting Improvement:</u> In our quest for quality awesomeness, we've learned that improvement knows no bounds. Embrace the cycle of continuous improvement, where every milestone becomes a stepping stone to greater heights. As one challenge is conquered, another awaits, and with each victory, we refine our skills and knowledge. Let us forever strive to surpass ourselves and keep the torch of improvement burning bright.

2. <u>Spreading the Joy of Quality:</u> We've discovered that joy and fun are potent catalysts for success. Embrace the joy of quality management and share it with others. Inspire new quality adventurers to embark on their journeys, passing down the wisdom and experiences we've gained. As mentors, let us nurture a new generation of quality heroes and heroines, eager to shape a better future.

3. <u>A Global Fellowship of Quality:</u> Quality knows no boundaries, and the pursuit of excellence unites us all. Connect with quality enthusiasts from all corners of the globe, sharing insights, successes, and challenges. Establish a global fellowship of quality, where diverse perspectives converge to create a world of quality innovation and progress.

4. <u>The Impact of Innovation:</u> Innovation has been the lifeblood of our quest for quality awesomeness. Let us continue to embrace the spirit of innovation in every endeavour. By pushing the boundaries of creativity, we'll uncover breakthroughs that

revolutionize quality management and redefine what's possible.

5. Embracing Diversity and Inclusion: As we forge ahead, let us never forget the strength in diversity and inclusion. Embrace the richness of perspectives, backgrounds, and experiences, as it empowers us to overcome challenges with greater resilience and creativity. Together, we'll create an inclusive world of quality, where every voice contributes to the symphony of improvement.

6. A Legacy of Inspiration: The legacy of quality awesomeness is not just about achievements; it's about the inspiration we leave behind. Share your stories of triumphs and setbacks, illuminating the path for others who tread a similar road. Be the guiding light that sparks courage and resilience in those who strive for excellence.

As we come to the end of this adventure, let us remember that the quest for quality awesomeness is eternal. Our pursuit of excellence knows no bounds, and with every challenge we conquer, we pave the way for a brighter future. Embrace the spirit of continuity, joy, and innovation, and let it guide you on your journey of ever-improving greatness.

I know that my quest doesn't end here. My legacy of quality awesomeness is just beginning. Go forth, inspire others, and forge an everlasting impact on the world of quality management. Together, we'll continue to shape a realm of excellence, leaving behind a lasting legacy that stands the test of time. May your journey be filled with triumphs, joy, and the relentless pursuit of quality awesomeness!

Chapter 13: Putting Humour into Practice: Exercises for Embracing Quality with a Grin

In this final section, we'll explore hands-on exercises and workshops designed to help you integrate humour and innovation into your quality management journey. These activities aim to inspire creative thinking, enhance team collaboration, and foster a culture of quality excellence with a touch of humour. Let's dive in!

Exercise 1: Humour Brainstorming

Objective: Encourage your team to brainstorm humorous solutions to common quality management challenges.

Instructions:

- Divide your team into small groups.
- Assign each group a specific quality-related challenge or scenario.
- Challenge each group to come up with a humorous solution or approach to tackle the challenge.
- After a set time, have each group present their humorous solution to the entire team.
- Discuss how these solutions could actually inspire innovative approaches to quality management.

Exercise 2: Quality Improvement Stand-Up

Objective: Promote open communication and problem-solving through humour-infused discussions.

Instructions:

- Gather your team in a casual setting.
- Have team members take turns presenting a humorous stand-up routine related to a recent quality challenge or improvement project.
- Encourage the use of light-hearted anecdotes and creative exaggerations.
- After each presentation, engage in a discussion about the underlying quality issue and potential solutions.
- Reflect on how humour can facilitate better communication and collaboration in problem-solving.

Workshop: Creating a Quality Comedy Club

Objective: Foster a supportive environment where team members can share quality-related humorous stories and insights.

Instructions:

- Set up a regular "Quality Comedy Club" session, either in-person or virtually.
- Invite team members to prepare and share their own humorous stories, anecdotes, or observations related to quality management.
- Encourage a positive and respectful atmosphere for sharing, where everyone feels comfortable contributing.
- Discuss the lessons or insights that can be drawn from these stories, enhancing the team's understanding of quality challenges and solutions.

Reflection: Humour Action Plan

Objective: Encourage readers to create a personalized action plan for incorporating humour into their quality management practices.

Instructions:

- Reflect on the insights and concepts discussed throughout the book.
- Identify specific areas in your quality management processes where humour could be applied effectively.
- Set concrete goals for incorporating humour, such as introducing a light-hearted icebreaker at team meetings or using humour to communicate important messages.
- Outline steps for implementing these goals and track your progress over time.

By engaging in these exercises and workshops, you'll be taking the first steps toward creating a workplace culture that embraces quality with a grin. Remember, humour is a powerful tool for enhancing creativity, reducing stress, and building stronger team dynamics. Embrace the journey, and let the power of laughter guide your path to quality excellence!

Conclusion: Embracing Quality Management with a Grin

As you reach the final pages of this book, you embark on a journey through the fascinating world of quality management, where humour and innovation intertwine to create a new perspective. You have discovered the power of laughter to improve team dynamics, to ignite creativity by evaluating different interests within the scope of diversity, and to improve the quality of your work. Along the way, you've experienced fictional characters, real-life leaders, and moments of laughter that illuminate the path to a more enjoyable and effective quality management journey.

Seriousness and hard work have their place in quality management, but the addition of humour and innovation brings a new dimension that can revolutionize your approach. As you've discovered, a well-timed joke, clever pun or playful activity can break down barriers, bridge communication gaps, and nurture a culture of collaboration and excellence.

Now you have the opportunity to begin your own quest for quality improvement, armed with insights, strategies, and a newfound appreciation for the value of humour. Whether you're a seasoned leader, dedicated team member, or aspiring quality advocate, the principles shared in this book are at your service to transform your workplace and beyond.

As you continue your journey, remember that "Innovation for Quality" is not just a phrase; It is a mindset that encourages you to view challenges as opportunities, smile at setbacks, and bring some creativity into every aspect of your business. By inviting humour and innovation into your quality management practices, you not only increase productivity and efficiency, but also nurture a positive and engaging work environment.

Armed with the tools of humour, the sword of innovation, move forward and continue to shape the world of quality management in your own unique and remarkable way. Let laughter be your ally, creativity your friend, and your pursuit of quality. Thank you for joining us in this exploration, and may your journey be filled with endless chuckles, limitless innovations, and a legacy of exceptional quality.

With his smiling face and heart full of joy…

AFTERWORD

Dear Reader,

Congratulations on completing your journey through "QUALITY WITH A GRIN EMBRACING HUMOR AND INNOVATION IN QUALITY MANAGEMENT" I hope you've enjoyed the humorous insights, innovative strategies, and practical tips that have been shared within these pages.

Your opinion matters to me! If you found this book valuable, I kindly ask for your support by leaving a review on Amazon. Your feedback not only helps me understand your thoughts on the book but also assists other readers in making informed decisions.

To share your thoughts, simply navigate to the book's page on Amazon and scroll down to the "Customer Reviews" section. Your comments and ratings contribute to the ongoing conversation around quality management and humor, and your input is highly appreciated.

Thank you for being a part of this journey. Your laughter, engagement, and dedication to quality improvement are what make this book truly special.

With gratitude,

Nur Simsir

Printed in Great Britain
by Amazon

28776318R00099